ABSTRACT

THE MEDIATING EFFECTS OF WORK-RELATED STRESS ON MENTORING
FUNCTIONS AND JOB ATTITUDE: A COMPARISON OF GENERAL AND
SPECIAL EDUCATION TEACHERS

Greg A. Rabenhorst, Ed.D.
Department of Leadership, Educational Psychology, and Foundations
Northern Illinois University, 2011
Rosita Lopez, Director

The current study is designed to investigate the mediating effects of work-related stress on the relationship between mentoring functions (i.e., career support, psychosocial support, and role modeling) and measures of job attitude (i.e., job satisfaction and organizational commitment). Mentoring is widely used as a means of assisting in the new teacher induction process across districts in the United States and Illinois in particular. Mentoring has been demonstrated to positively affect job outcomes such as job satisfaction and organizational commitment. These two specific outcome measures have also been predictive of retention in the field. Teacher attrition is a concern among public school districts due to the resources devoted to recruitment, hiring, inducting, and developing new teachers. The role of stress in new teachers' lives also impacts their job attitude and decisions to stay in the field. Educational research has identified differences in the effects of mentoring outcomes between general education and special education teachers. Research outside of education has established that work-related stress, as measured by role ambiguity and role conflict, mediates the relationship between mentoring functions and job outcomes.

This study analyzed the self-report data of 260 teacher participants representing multiple districts across Northern Illinois. Responses were analyzed to determine the mediating effects of work-related stress on the relationship between mentoring functions and job attitude. Data analyses revealed that most mentor function variables were significantly negatively correlated with both role conflict and role ambiguity, suggesting that increased support from one's mentor was associated with less work-related stress. Likewise, each of the mentor function variables was significantly positively associated with both job attitude variables, indicating that increased support from one's mentor was associated with increased job satisfaction and organizational commitment. Finally, both work-related stress variables were significantly negatively associated with the job attitude variables, indicating that higher scores on role conflict and ambiguity were associated with lower scores on job satisfaction and organizational commitment. SEM analyses indicated that role conflict and role ambiguity partially mediated the relationship between Mentor Functions and Job Attitude but did not completely eliminate the direct relationship.

NORTHERN ILLINOIS UNIVERSITY

DEKALB, ILLINOIS

DECEMBER 2011

THE MEDIATING EFFECTS OF WORK-RELATED STRESS ON MENTORING

FUNCTIONS AND JOB ATTITUDE: A COMPARISON OF GENERAL AND

SPECIAL EDUCATION TEACHERS

BY

GREG A. RABENHORST

A DISSERTATION SUBMITTED TO THE GRADUATE SCHOOL

IN PARTIAL FULFILLMENTOF THE REQUIREMENTS

FOR THE DEGREE

DOCTOR OF EDUCATION

DEPARTMENT OF

LEADERSHIP, EDUCATIONAL PSYCHOLOGY, AND FOUNDATIONS

Doctoral Director:
Rosita Lopez

UMI Number: 3495035

Dissertation Publishing

UMI 3495035

ACKNOWLEDGMENTS

I owe a significant amount of my academic success to my very best friend, Dr. Mandy Rabenhorst. Without her unfailing love and support, my spirit for pursuing continued advanced academic study would not exist, and the quality of my work would certainly be noticeably less stellar. Mandy's analytic skills are beyond comparison to others as she has challenged me to think about and understand information and data in more thorough ways. In addition to her intelligence and ability to teach and explain, Mandy has been a foundation of personal and emotional support for me. She has stood by me through the most difficult of personal circumstances, and without her, this piece of academic work would not have found its way to completion. I am proud to have shared so much of my life with her. I love you, Mandy.

To my boys, Tad and Link. My goal in all of this was to get this degree done before you were old enough to remember the amount of time I was away from you. I now recognize that no matter what age you were or are there is nothing more important to me than watching you grow, advance, and mature. I hope I show you that every day. I also desire for you to always recognize the importance of education and intellectual stimulation. Even though I want that for you, I want for you to be yourselves even more, even if that means you don't have advanced degrees in your future. I love you for the joy you bring to my life and to others' lives. Thank you for sacrificing so that I could attain this goal.

I owe a great deal of gratitude to those who have been of academic and professional support to me. First, Dr. Rosita Lopez has been a cheerleader of sorts to me and has been nothing but encouraging in the completion of this dissertation. I appreciate her dedication to the field and her willingness to work with me as the director of this project. Likewise, I am grateful to the other members of my committee (Drs. Jacobson, Saban, and Burton), who have given up their personal and professional time to improve my work and assist me in completing my degree. Professionally, I would not have reached this stage without the encouragement and support of Dr. Brad Hawk and Dr. Ron Cope. These educational leaders saw potential in me that even I didn't imagine and persuaded me to take on this challenge well before I thought I was ready. I owe my current career advancement to these gentlemen and will never forget the ways they have assisted me.

Finally, my ultimate success is only because of my foundational belief in Christ. God has various challenges, successes, and failures in store for all of us. I trust in Him in all that I do and know that His purpose will be served through my work in education.

DEDICATION

to Tad & Link

TABLE OF CONTENTS

Chapter	Page

LIST OF TABLES

LIST OF FIGURES

LIST OF APPENDICES

CHAPTER 1

INTRODUCTION

Rationale

The teaching profession has been plagued with high levels of attrition,

particularly among teachers just beginning their careers. While all occupations

experience some degree of attrition, educational research indicates that as many as

fifty percent of new teachers leave the field within the first five years (Smith &

Ingersoll, 2004). With policy changes and demographic changes occurring in several

areas of the country, certain districts constantly recruit for new teaching positions,

which compounds the problem attrition creates for the field (Feaster, 2002). Specific

problems associated with being a first-year teacher appear to increase the likelihood of

attrition early in the career. These problems include difficulties managing time and

resources, problems motivating and managing students, issues related to

differentiation of instruction, difficulties assessing and analyzing student progress,

insufficient training for communicating with parents, and problems communicating

with colleagues and administrators (Gehrke & Murri, 2006; Quinn & Andrews, 2004;

Whitaker, 2003).

While keeping teachers in the profession has proven to be problematic, the

concerns with retention of special education teachers are even more profound.

Researchers estimate that nine percent or more of special education teachers leave the field annually and that these educators continue to leave more often year after year when compared to general education teachers (Boe, Bobbit, & Cook, 1997; Boyer & Gillespie, 2000; Fore, Martin, & Bender, 2002; White & Mason, 2006). In addition to the specific problems experienced by general education teachers, special educators face unique stressors, including caseloads/class loads, burdensome paperwork, lack of planning time, multiple job responsibilities, and limited support from teachers and administrators, all of whom contribute to their decision to leave the field (Fore et al., 2002; Gehrke & Murri, 2006; Schlichte, Yssel, & Merbler, 2005; Thornton, Peltier, & Medina, 2007; Whitaker, 2003; White & Mason, 2006).

Induction and mentoring have been identified as means of reducing teacher attrition and providing support for first-year teachers (Feaster, 2002; Fletcher & Barrett, 2004; White & Mason, 2006). Induction consists of programming aimed at supporting, providing guidance to, and orienting new employees into the profession. Mentoring is the personal relationship that exists between an employee and his/her identified veteran teacher mentor (Smith & Ingersoll, 2004). The literature distinguishes between two distinct types of mentoring, facilitated and spontaneous (Egan & Song, 2008). The former consists of a more formal, structured mentoring process, while the latter encompasses the more unstructured, impromptu mentoring relationship that may exist between a mentor and protégé.

Among its many benefits, mentoring has been found to aid first-year teachers with the logistics of starting in the profession as well as socializing and acclimating these teachers into a school's culture (Smith & Ingersoll, 2004). In addition to logistical support, research shows that mentors provide early-career teachers with instructional support, systems support (e.g., paperwork), and emotional support (Fletcher & Barrett, 2004; Scherff & Hahs-Vaughn, 2008). Although less well established, this body of literature also indicates that student achievement is positively associated with improved performance demonstrated by first-year teachers as a result of having been mentored. Research specifically studying the effects of mentoring on special education personnel suggests that mentoring positively affects both career and psychosocial outcomes. Much of this research points to factors such as having a special educator as a mentor, frequent, informal contact with the mentor, and a nonevaluative relationship with the mentor that lead to better measured outcomes for these teachers (Boyer & Gillespie, 2000; Whitaker, 2000a; Whitaker, 2000b; Kennedy & Burnstein, 2004; Schlichte et al., 2005; White & Mason, 2006; Thornton et al., 2007).

The broader literature also has identified connections between mentoring and psychosocial outcomes such as job satisfaction, organizational commitment, and work-related stress (Allen, Poteet, Eby, Lentz, & Lima, 2004; Billingsley, 1992; Egan & Song, 2008; Kammeyer-Mueller & Judge, 2008; Lankau, Carlson, & Nielson, 2006; Seibert, 1999; Waters, 2004). Mentoring has been linked with increased job satisfaction of both the mentor and the mentee. Protégés involved in mentoring programs show higher levels of organizational commitment and person-organization fit compared to protégés not involved in mentoring programs (Allen et al., 2004).

Similarly, Seibert (1999) found that facilitated mentoring was related to reports of reduced work-role stress. A study by Egan and Song (2008) experimentally compared groups of protégés participating in each type of mentoring (facilitated v. spontaneous) and found similarities in psychosocial outcomes; however, they found that those individuals in the spontaneous mentoring group received more career support (e.g., enhancement of career standing) than those in the facilitated group. This body of research also reveals a relationship between work stressors such as role conflict/role ambiguity and job satisfaction, commitment, and retention.

Unfortunately to date, much of the research investigating the relationship between mentoring and psychosocial outcomes has been conducted outside of the educational setting. Indeed, what appears to be lacking in the education literature is empirical research investigating the connection between perceived outcomes (i.e., work-related stress, satisfaction, and commitment) and mentoring. Given the higher rates of attrition seen in special education when compared to general education (Boyer & Gillespie, 2000; White & Mason, 2006), it stands to reason that the quality and type of mentoring may have a differential impact on these teachers' decision to stay in the job or profession. As mentioned previously, special educators are burdened with paperwork, multiple responsibilities in their role, and the most behaviorally challenging students (Fore et al., 2002; Singh & Billingsley, 1996; Whitaker, 2003). These studies demonstrate that the work-related stress felt by special educators is due in part to lack of support from peers and administrators and feelings of isolation. Studies by Whitaker (2000a) and Schlichte et al. (2005) found that special educators were more satisfied with spontaneous mentoring compared to facilitated mentoring. This limited research suggests that specific stressors unique to special educators may be alleviated more through spontaneous mentoring rather than a more formal mentoring model, although this does not suggest that these teachers receive no benefit from formal mentoring. In addition, Whitaker's (2003) investigation determined that the amount of assistance needed by new special educators was far greater than the amount of assistance received through mentoring. Taken together, this research suggests that the more mentoring available, the better.

Among other stressors such as insufficient planning time, lack of programmatic structure, and loss of teacher control, research involving special educators has demonstrated that two organizational conditions exist which serve as a major source of stress on the job: role conflict and role ambiguity (Wisniewski & Gargiulo, 1997). Higher rates of role conflict and role ambiguity have been found among special educators when compared to a group of general educators (Billingsley & Cross, 1992). Lankau, Carlson, and Nielson (2006) identified in their sample of business management graduates that increased psychosocial support through mentoring was associated with fewer stressors. Specifically, Lankau et al. identified that role ambiguity and role conflict served as significant mediators in the relationship between psychosocial support and job attitudes (as measured by satisfaction and commitment) as well as role modeling and job attitude. No similar study has been identified utilizing samples of educators to determine the mediational relationship of stress between functions of mentoring and important psychosocial outcome measures such as job satisfaction and organizational commitment, both of which have been demonstrated to play a significant role in teacher retention.

Research Questions

The current study specifically aimed to identify factors related to the problem of retention of teachers and special education teachers, in particular, in the field. Teachers within their second to tenth year in the profession were sought for participation in the study. The researcher surveyed probationary and tenured general education and special education teacher participants to ascertain information about the type of mentoring program they were involved in during their first and second years of teaching. Participants completed psychosocial outcome measures to determine the potential effects of mentoring on measures of job attitude including job satisfaction, organizational commitment, and work-related stress.

This study proposed that reductions in work-related stress, as measured by role conflict and role ambiguity, mediate the positive relationship between mentoring and protégés' attitudes. The current research sought to identify if these role stressors mediate the relationships between the mentoring functions (i.e., career support, psychosocial support, and role modeling) and job satisfaction and organizational commitment, both of which are well-established outcomes of mentoring. Additionally, analyses were conducted to determine if there is a significant difference in the strength of the mediational effects of stress on outcomes of job attitude between general education teachers and special education teachers. The study was guided by the following research questions:

1.   Do reductions in work-related stress, as measured by role conflict and role ambiguity, account for (i.e., mediate) the positive relationship between mentoring functions and protégé job attitudes? This question was guided by the following hypotheses:

a.   The relationship between career support and job satisfaction is mediated by (i.e., will be weakened after accounting for) role conflict.

b.   The relationship between career support and job satisfaction is mediated by (i.e., will be weakened after accounting for) role ambiguity.

c.   The relationship between career support and organizational commitment is mediated by (i.e., will be weakened after accounting for) role conflict.

d.   The relationship between career support and organizational commitment is mediated by (i.e., will be weakened after accounting for) role ambiguity.

e.   The relationship between psychosocial support and job satisfaction is mediated by (i.e., will be weakened after accounting for) role conflict.

f.   The relationship between psychosocial support and job satisfaction is mediated by (i.e., will be weakened after accounting for) role ambiguity.

g.   The relationship between psychosocial support and organizational commitment is mediated by (i.e., will be weakened after accounting for) role conflict.

h.   The relationship between psychosocial support and organizational commitment is mediated by (i.e., will be weakened after accounting for) role ambiguity.

i.   The relationship between role modeling and job satisfaction is mediated by (i.e., will be weakened after accounting for) role conflict.

j.   The relationship between role modeling and job satisfaction is mediated by (i.e., will be weakened after accounting for) role ambiguity.

k.   The relationship between role modeling and organizational commitment is mediated by (i.e., will be weakened after accounting for) role conflict.

l.   The relationship between role modeling and organizational commitment is mediated by (i.e., will be weakened after accounting for) role ambiguity.

2.   Is there a significant difference in the mediating effects of stressors (i.e., role conflict and role ambiguity) on outcomes of job attitude between general and special education teachers?

Definitions of Terms

Career support: This established function of mentoring leads to the mentee becoming an independent and successful professional through the teaching of job-related functions such as sponsorship, exposure, coaching, and assignment of challenging tasks. Career support is also referred to as vocational support in the professional literature.

Facilitated mentoring: This form of mentoring is a formal process of mentoring which is guided by a set of external expectations including but not limited to expectations for participation, meeting times, and or discussion topics.

Job satisfaction: Job satisfaction is defined as an affective reaction of an employee regarding his or her liking or happiness toward work or employment.

Induction: Breaux and Wong (2003) define induction to include "all of the things that are done to support and train new teachers and acculturate them to teaching, including the responsibilities, missions, and philosophies of their districts and schools" (2003, p. 5).

Mentoring: Mentoring is defined as a support structure for new employees of an organization. The structure consists of a mentor who is available for the protégée or mentee on a formal and/or informal basis with consistent and regular contact where the mentor can provide knowledge, input, or advice. Within the field of education, Hope (1999) regards mentoring as a systematic process with the intention of a mentor assisting a new teacher with professional growth and development and of "engaging in collegial conversation about the work of teaching" (p. 54).

Organizational commitment: Organizational commitment is a conceptualization of job attitude. It is a psychological bond that binds an employee to the organization.

Psychosocial support: Psychosocial support is an established function of mentoring which leads to the mentee's sense of competence and effectiveness in the job through the mentor's counseling of the mentee about job-related anxieties and relationships.

Role ambiguity: A dimension of work-stress which refers to the feeling an employee has when he or she has been provided insufficient information to perform required roles and responsibilities adequately.

Role conflict: A dimension of work-stress which refers to the phenomenon that occurs when information given to an employee about roles and responsibilities conflicts with the realities of the employee's daily duties and responsibilities.

Role modeling: Role modeling is an established function of mentoring where the mentor demonstrates job-related behaviors and knowledge.

Spontaneous mentoring: This form of mentoring is an informal process of mentoring which may include unstructured, impromptu, one-on-one support from a mentor to the protégée.

Statistical mediation: A statistical model that seeks to identify and determine the mechanism underlying the relationship between an independent variable (i.e., a mentoring function) and a dependent variable (i.e., job attitude). This third explanatory, underlying mechanism (i.e., work-related stressor) is referred to as the mediator variable and helps to clarify the nature of the relationship between the independent and dependent variables.

Work-related stress: This term refers to the amount of stress perceived by an employee due to the nature of his or her work and may include such stressors as role conflict and role ambiguity.

Significance of the Study

Results of the current study regarding the relationships between mentoring functions, work-related stress, and job attitude can provide school districts with information about how to better provide support to beginning general education and special education teachers. Identifying aspects of the relationship between mentoring and psychosocial outcome measures and how this may impact the potential for teacher retention is critical in developing effective induction and mentoring programs that will help keep educators, particularly special educators, in their current positions.

Summary

Teacher retention in the field is a significant concern for school districts due to the cost of replacing teachers and the impact turnover may potentially have on student outcomes. Induction programs and mentoring in particular have been identified in the human resource literature, as well as the education literature, as a means of helping first-year employees adapt and adjust to their new professions and to their new employing organizations. There is a significant body of literature that suggests teacher retention is affected by psychosocial outcomes such as job satisfaction and organizational commitment. Studies have shown a relationship between mentoring and higher levels of job satisfaction and organizational commitment. While teacher stress and burnout have been studied by many researchers, there appears to be limited analysis of the impact work-related stress has on psychosocial outcomes that are likely impacted by mentoring. Literature from the human resource and vocational management fields suggests that work-related stress serves as a mediating variable between the identified functions (e.g., types of support) of mentoring and important predictive outcomes of retention such as job satisfaction and organizational commitment. Identifying the role stress plays in a first-year teacher's professional experience may shed light on these teachers' perceived benefit from functions of mentoring and their rated job satisfaction and organizational commitment. The stress literature has also identified factors unique to special educators; therefore, a comparison of the mediating effects of stress on mentoring functions and measures of job attitude were made between general education and special education teachers.

Chapter 2 is an extensive review of the literature which outlines the importance of mentoring first-year employees and why there is a unique need for mentoring in education. The struggles of beginning teachers are explored as well as the differential experiences of general and special education teachers. Research studies are explored which indicate that mentoring serves to alleviate some of the negative experiences first-year teachers face. Studies that have demonstrated a relationship between lower rates of attrition and being involved in a mentoring program are also reviewed.

Specific functions and types of mentoring are described along with research studies that suggest specific psychosocial outcomes are related to specific functions of mentoring. The psychosocial outcomes of job satisfaction, organizational commitment, and work-related stress are outlined as well as their connections to job retention. Involvement in mentoring programs is related to higher levels of job satisfaction and organizational commitment and lower levels of work-related stress, and more positive levels of job satisfaction and organization are related to increased retention in the field. The literature review examined how mentoring functions may lead to improved job attitude by reducing work-related stress.

CHAPTER 2

LITERATURE REVIEW

Beginning a new job or career can be an overwhelming experience for a new employee regardless of the type of position. Feeling anxious about the unknown is common for many, and having someone to provide guidance and direction can help alleviate anxiety for the new employee. The vocational literature is abundant with research demonstrating the positive effects of mentoring on new employees in a variety of fields. Seibert (1999) reported that from one-third to two-thirds of employees in a variety of employment positions are engaged in a mentoring relationship. This literature defines mentoring in an assortment of ways. The term *mentor* has its roots in Greek mythology, which describes it as "a relationship between a younger adult and an older, more experienced adult who helps the younger individual learn to navigate the adult world and the world of work" (Allen, Poteet, Eby, Lentz, & Lima, 2004, p. 127). In employment settings, mentoring has been defined as an intense working relationship between the senior member of an organization and the junior member of an organization (Waters, 2004).

The mentoring relationship also may be considered developmental since it is geared toward career advancement and psychological growth for the protégé, or the person being mentored (Seibert, 1999). Others add that the mentoring relationship contains no supervisory or evaluative component (Kammeyer-Mueller & Judge, 2008). Specifically in education, the definition of mentoring considers the mentor an educational companion who helps a new teacher solve problems in the classroom and learn about school policies, rules, and other logistical matters but who does not evaluate the teacher's performance in a formal way (Fletcher & Barrett, 2004). Regardless of the perspective, a commonality among definitions appears to be the idea that a new employee is "learning the ropes" from a more experienced, veteran employee.

The literature on mentoring suggests that there is an inherent link between the mentoring relationship and career success. This assumed link is based primarily on social learning theory, which explains that modeling the behavior of the veteran or senior organizational member leads to career success on the part of the mentee (Bandura, 1977). Protégés observe the behaviors of their mentors, which helps develop skills and increase their own self-efficacy. This process allows for vicarious learning on the job. In addition to specific skill building, the protégé learns how to gain entry into the formal and informal social networks of the organization. Without such guidance and assistance, the less experienced person in an organization may not acquire the behaviors that lead to success within the organization (Allen et al., 2004; Lankau et al., 2006).

Authors such has Wong (2004) find it important to distinguish mentoring from induction. Induction is a program of professional development for a newer employee in an organization, and mentoring is one subcomponent of the induction program.

Although Wong and others find induction to be a critical factor in retaining teachers to the profession, mentoring is the focus of the current research as a separate entity to be studied. Much of the literature does not adequately make the distinction between mentoring and induction; however, the review of relevant studies attempts to analyze the facets of mentoring and its effect on teachers' psychosocial outcomes that may lead to their decision to remain in the profession.

The Need for Mentoring in Education

Education has been impacted by demographic and policy trends which have led to an increase in the need for new teachers in recent decades. Student enrollment increases, teacher retirement increases, efforts to reduce class size, and a decrease in certified teacher availability have resulted in many districts looking for new teachers (Feaster, 2002). This general increase in need has been coupled with a problem of teacher attrition. Although all occupations experience some degree of attrition, educational research has indicated that as many as fifty percent of new teachers leave the field within the first five years (Ingersoll & Kralik, 2004; Smith & Ingersoll, 2004). Teacher retention has been a consistent concern in the United States for a variety of reasons. Gehrke and Murri (2006) provide a synopsis of the problems associated with first-year teachers which have an impact on retention and provide the basis for the need for mentoring programs. First-year teachers often struggle with obtaining and managing time and resources; motivating students; managing classroom behavior and discipline; gaining information about school rules and policies;

differentiating instruction to all individuals; communicating with parents; and finding emotional support systems.

When compared to veteran teachers, beginning teachers struggle with managing classroom behavior and dealing with parent interactions (Melnick & Meister, 2008). Although not significantly different from veterans, beginning teachers also struggle with time management related to workload. In addition, first-year teachers report needing assistance with instruction and curriculum; planning, organizing, and managing instruction; assessing student progress and analyzing forms of data; communicating with colleagues and administrators/supervisors; managing the environment; and dealing with student needs and interests (Quinn & Andrews, 2004; Whitaker, 2003). Although perhaps difficult for all teachers, these needs and problems are often exacerbated for first-year teachers because they often end up working with the most difficult populations. Fletcher and Barrett (2004) reported that less experienced teachers are more likely to start out teaching in lower-achieving schools with students often considered more difficult to teach; therefore, the demands placed on these new teachers are even higher than when compared to experienced teachers. The problem is then cyclical because once these inexperienced teachers gain experience, they are likely to leave these schools for jobs in higher performing districts.

With all of these identified problems and needs, mentoring has been established as a means to alleviate or minimize the negative effects on first-year teachers. The broader research field establishes that attrition is reduced by mentoring programs that include goals for socialization of new employees into the organizational culture and support for career development (Egan & Song, 2008). Odell and Ferraro (1992) found retention rates of two cohorts of teachers to be 83-86% four years after having participated in an induction and mentoring program. Participation in mentoring and induction activities that included networking decreased the likelihood of English teachers leaving the profession by about 90% compared to teachers who did not participate in such activities (Scherff & Hahs-Vaughn, 2008). In a qualitative study examining the effects of peer mentoring on beginning science teachers, Forbes (2004) concluded that professional decisions were enhanced, and skills associated with classroom management, curricular planning, and interacting with colleagues/administrators were improved.

In their quantitative research synthesis, Kammeyer-Mueller and Judge (2008) found that mentoring is an important predictor of many positive career outcomes such as performance and satisfaction. Even after personality and other career outcome variables such as tenure and education were held constant, other benefits of mentoring, such as satisfaction, were found to be modest. These career outcomes are particularly important in that they have been established as predictive of retention in the field. Specific to the field of education, Ingersoll and Kralik (2004) reviewed 150 empirical studies of induction and mentoring programs and identified ten studies published between 1987 and 2003 that met strict criteria for inclusion in their study. These authors concluded that assistance to new teachers and teacher mentoring programs specifically have an overall positive effect on teachers and retention. However, the conclusions drawn by Ingersoll and Kralik have been criticized for weaknesses inherent in their study, which included no control for other factors affecting outcomes and significant variation in programs studied (Fletcher, Strong, & Villar, 2008).

Student achievement is of particular importance in education, and as Wong states, "What the teacher knows and can do in the classroom is the most important factor resulting in student achievement" (2004, p. 41). The impact of new teachers on student achievement has been difficult, if not impossible, to study experimentally. Fletcher and Barrett (2004) studied the achievement gains of students taught by novice teachers and compared those to the achievement gains of students taught by mid-career and veteran teachers. Although there were demographic differences for the three groups, classes taught by the novice teachers showed comparable gain scores to those taught by veteran teachers. Interestingly, classes taught by mid-career teachers showed the highest achievement gain scores compared to the other two groups. Because teacher induction and mentoring generally has not been around for more than twenty years, those mid-career teachers were more likely to experience mentoring support while those veteran teachers would have had little or no induction or mentoring. The authors concluded that the combination of mentoring and teaching experience has a more significant impact on student achievement than either factor alone. Fletcher and Strong (2009) conducted another study investigating the effects of mentoring on achievement. In this study, twenty-eight teachers were assigned either a site-based mentor or a full-release mentor. The results indicated that students associated with full-release mentors had better achievement gains than students associated with site-based mentors. Fletcher et al. (2008) indicated that mentoring programs may have a positive effect on student achievement if the mentoring program has frequent (e.g., at least weekly) meetings, and individuals serving as mentors are fully released from the classroom to provide mentoring to a group of new teachers.

In order to study teacher perceptions, Fletcher and Barrett (2004) surveyed teachers teaching in grades 2-6 in a California school district of more than 15,000 students. The survey results revealed that the vast majority of new teachers (98.6% of those surveyed) believed that mentors aided them in improving instruction and teaching. Additionally, 92.8% believed mentors aided them in managing classroom behavior, 88.6% found benefits of mentoring in assessing student skill acquisition, 87.1% identified mentoring as helping them to differentiate instruction, and more than 95.0% of new teachers found their mentors to be helpful in learning to work effectively with a culturally diverse range of students. The results indicated that both achievement gains and teacher perceptions establish the foundation for mentoring as a plausible intervention to assist new teachers and as a mechanism to reduce teacher attrition.

Functions and Types of Mentoring

The literature reveals three distinct functions or types of support served by mentoring: career (also referred to as vocational support), psychosocial, and role modeling. The career function serves to enhance the mentee's career standing and includes such areas as sponsorship, exposure/visibility, coaching, protection, and provision of challenging assignments. The career function is enhanced by the mentor's experience, seniority, and potential influence in the organization. The psychosocial function of mentoring helps to shape professional identity and competence and includes acceptance and confirmation, counseling, and friendship (Allen et al., 2004; Lankau, Carlson, & Nielson, 2006; Seibert, 1999). Kammeyer-Mueller and Judge (2008) elaborated on these two functions by stating that career functions enhance human capital by linking protégés to powerful individuals in the organization, and psychosocial functions help to alleviate protégé uncertainty by providing acceptance to the protégé. Allen et al. identified career and psychosocial functions as the "primary distinct and reliable overarching operationalizations of mentoring provided" (p. 128). Role modeling refers to the act of the mentor demonstrating behaviors and relaying knowledge, which leads to respect and admiration from the protégé toward the mentor (Lankau et al., 2006). In much of the research literature, role modeling is frequently included with the psychosocial functions of mentoring; however, Lankau et al. and Castro, Scandura, and Williams (2006) identified role modeling as an independent function of mentoring.

Research suggests that both career and psychosocial functions are often served within the same mentoring relationship (Noe, 1988). Noe surveyed 139 teacher protégés and found that mentored teachers received both career and psychosocial outcomes from their mentors; however, career mentoring was received less often than psychosocial mentoring. Specifically, protégés frequently reported obtaining feelings of acceptance and confirmation, being provided a forum for exploring personal and professional dilemmas, and receiving beneficial feedback. In contrast, they less frequently reported receiving behaviors associated with career outcomes such as protection, exposure and visibility, and sponsorship. While the reasons for this difference were not analyzed by the study, the fact that some of these career outcomes may take more time to acquire could potentially explain the lower frequency of reporting found in the study.

In their meta-analysis, Allen and colleagues (2004) found that both the psychosocial and career functions of mentoring were positively related to organizational outcomes such as job satisfaction and organizational commitment, while career functions were also associated with more objective career outcomes such as compensation and promotions. The latter finding was reported to have a small effect size. Egan and Song (2008) summarized these findings on mentoring functions by suggesting that both career and psychosocial functions of mentoring help to make clear the effectiveness of mentoring as an intervention. Allen et al.'s findings also suggest that the quality of the mentor-protégé relationship influences the psychosocial functions of mentoring. Agreement between the protégé and mentor on their relationship leads to openness regarding feedback from one another, which could result in adjustments of attitude and behavior that may be needed in the mentoring relationship (Waters, 2004). Waters found that stronger agreement in the mentoring relationship led to stronger satisfaction with the relationship as well as with the job in general. The results of this same study suggest that organizations must find ways to promote the informal relationship that develops between a mentor and protégé. More frequent, informal interactions between the two fosters a stronger relationship, which is thought to be the mechanism by which the new employee experiences positive outcomes, such as organizational commitment and job satisfaction (Waters, 2004).

In addition to serving different functions, mentoring also may differ in its delivery or implementation. Some organizations may employ an informal process (i.e., spontaneous mentoring), while others may utilize a formal process (i.e., facilitated mentoring). Whereas spontaneous mentoring is not guided by external expectations, facilitated mentoring is guided by set expectations for participation, meeting times, and/or discussion topics (Egan & Song, 2008). Much of the research literature, particularly in educational settings, does not differentiate which type of mentoring was employed when studying the quantitative or qualitative effects of mentoring. Authors such as Strong (2005) indicate that mentoring programs vary considerably among districts, with some being highly formal to others being highly informal. Programs with a fully comprehensive support system for beginning teachers may include a full-time highly trained mentor with a caseload of mentees while the majority of others may include an assigned teacher mentor who is provided little, if any, compensation, training, or release time.

One noneducational study which did examine differences between spontaneous, facilitated, and nonmentored groups found that those employees in spontaneous mentoring relationships reported the highest levels of organization socialization and satisfaction, followed by those in facilitated mentoring relationships who, in turn, reported higher levels than those in the nonmentored group (Chao, Walz,

& Gardner, 1992). The authors concluded that spontaneous and facilitated mentoring programs result in comparable psychosocial outcomes but that career support was received more frequently in the spontaneous mentoring group. Egan and Song (2008) were among the first to systematically measure facilitated mentoring. Compared to nonmentored employees, employees who were in a facilitated mentoring program reported higher job satisfaction, organizational commitment, person-organization fit, and performance ratings. However, because their study did not include a spontaneous mentoring group, additional research is needed to examine the differential effects of facilitated versus spontaneous mentoring.

Components of a Quality Mentoring Program

Much has been written about what should be included in a highly effective mentoring program or what elements of the mentor-protégé relationship will lead to greater career outcomes. Some authors indicate that the mentorship should include role-taking experiences, reflection after real experiences, personal and professional support, and continuity of the mentor (Feaster, 2002). The matching of mentor to protégé has been deemed critical (Fletcher & Barrett, 2004; Kilburg & Hancock, 2006). Selecting a mentor who is working in the same building as the mentee, has teaching experience at the same grade level or in the same subject matter, has a strong willingness to work with a new teacher, and has strong interpersonal skills increases the likelihood of there being a good match. An additional critical, yet often overlooked, factor that will positively impact mentoring outcomes is ensuring adequate time for the mentor and protégé to work together. Emotional support and communication between the mentor and protégé also affect the quality of the mentoring relationship (Kilburg & Hancock, 2006). Fletcher and Barrett indicated that in order to be successful, the mentor must help the protégé interact with colleagues in the educational community and facilitate involvement in professional development activities.

Perhaps just as important as knowing what does work is knowing what does not work. Qualitative studies, such as those completed by Quinn and Andrews (2004) and Kilburg and Hancock (2006), reveal factors that have made mentoring unsuccessful as reported by protégés involved in the mentoring process. Through the collection of data over a two-year period from 149 mentoring teams, specific factors were identified as recurring problems in mentoring relationships and programs. These recurring problems included lacking time for observing and meeting, having a mentor in a different school or subject area, lacking emotional support, and poor coaching and communication skills (Kilburg & Hancock). Across the two years of their study, lack of time was the factor most consistently perceived to be a problem impacting the mentorship. Quinn and Andrews (2004) completed phone interviews with 57 teachers to identify what components in their mentoring program were lacking. From these interviews general themes appeared, including a lack of proper orientation to policies and procedures; insufficient information regarding building processes, materials, and resources; no protocols for setting up parent conferences; insufficient information about turning in grades or attendance; and lack of direction with regard to disciplinary procedures. Generally, this study indicated that schools and school leaders need to commit more time to properly orienting first-year teachers. Similarly, Fletcher and Barrett (2004) surveyed their study participants and concluded that in order to be successful, a mentor-based induction program must help new teachers acclimate to the culture of a school. This acclimation to school culture includes providing teachers with the opportunity to observe other teachers, guiding interactions with other educators in the building, and encouraging interactions with educators outside of the school.

Special Concerns for Special Education

In 2000, the Council for Exception Children (CEC) reported a serious national shortage of special education teachers in the United States. In addition to the shortage, the attrition rate of special education teachers is significant and adds to the shortage in the field. Available data indicate that special education teachers not only leave more often than their general education counterparts after the first year, but they continue to leave more often year after year compared to general education teachers in their cohorts (Boyer & Gillespie, 2000; White & Mason, 2006). Research has been conducted since at least the 1980s to determine the extent to which teacher attrition and turnover has occurred both with general education teachers and special education teachers. Boe and colleagues (Boe, Bobbitt, & Cook, 1997; Boe, Bobbitt, Cook, & Weber, 1997) studied the attrition and transfer of teachers in public schools following the 1987-1988 school year. In their analyses, results indicated higher annual turnover for special education teachers than general education teachers. The results of surveys completed by a national sample of 4,812 public school teachers indicated that almost 6% of the general education teachers left teaching between the 1987-88 and 1988-89 school years while nearly 8% of the special education teachers left teaching during the same time. In terms of transferring from one public school to another, 13% of special educators compared to 7% of general educators left their positions for another. These authors reported that when turnover included school reassignment, migration, and exit attrition, 21% of special educators left the school in one year.

Additional educational research has occurred in the 1990s and 2000s where researchers have sought to identify the rates at which educators either leave the field or transfer to a new position. Luekens and colleagues (2004) analyzed data gathered from the Teacher Follow-Up Survey (TFS) collected by the National Center for Education Statistics (NCES) from the 1999-2000 and 2000-2001 school years. This analysis indicated that 7.4% of public school teachers left the teaching field while an additional 7.7% moved to a different school, resulting in a total of 15.1% teacher attrition or migration at the school level. Further analysis of these data by Luekens et al. estimated that the rate of leaving teaching was 25.5% during the first three years, 32.0% during the first four years, and 38.5% during the first five years. Specific to special education, McKnab (1995) analyzed the rates of attrition of special education teachers in Kansas compared to national samples for the 1993-1994 school year and found that 9.0% - 10.0% of these teachers did not return to their positions the following school year.

Boe, Cook, and Sunderland (2008) analyzed differences in attrition and transfer rates between general and special education teachers from the 1991-1992 through 2000-2001 school years. Using three versions of the National Center for Education Statistics' Schools and Staff Surveys, these authors identified in general that nationwide teacher turnover was high, as 22.0% - 23.0% of public school special educators and general educators either left teaching, switched teaching areas, or migrated to a different school. This study included teaching area transfer as part of the turnover, which is unique to most studies researching the topic and likely explains why the percent of turnover is higher in their study. Over the nine-year period of time studied, Boe and colleagues found that the rate of turnover increased by more than a third. In terms of group differences, teacher attrition in special education appeared to be relatively equivalent in magnitude to that in general education during the 1990s; however, although attrition was quite similar between the groups in the early 1990s, the rates increased more over time for special educators than general educators. When analyzing the data from the 2000-2001 school year, 8.7% of special educators had exited the profession compared to 7.2% of general educators. Additionally, over the course of the entire time studied, more than twice as many special education teachers with 13 to 24 years of experience left teaching when compared to general educators with the same level of experience. With regard to school migration (i.e., transferring from one school to another), special educators within their first three years were significantly more likely to migrate than general educators within their first three years, 19.3% versus 13.1%, respectively.

The most recently found study examining teacher attrition and mobility was completed based on data from the 2004-2005 school year (Marvel, Lyter, Peltola, Strizek, & Morton, 2006). Of over three million public school teachers tracked, 8.0% moved to a different school, and 8.0% left the profession. Of those teachers under age 30, about 15.0% moved to another school, while 9.0% left teaching. When comparing the 2004-2005 school year to previous years, the data indicated an increase in both movers and leavers over time. Data for assignment fields in education revealed that special educators were more likely than general educators to both move to another position and leave the profession during the 2004-2005 school year, with 11.1% moving and 10.0% leaving. In comparison, when combining the general education categories of general elementary, arts/music, English/language arts, mathematics, natural sciences, and social sciences, only 7.6% of teachers in these groups moved, while an additional 7.6% left.

Although the data is subject to differences in analyses conducted by various researchers, there is substantial evidence that teacher attrition is a problem and that the problem is larger for special education than general education. Some authors have also indicated that the attrition in special education is even greater in urban districts (Fore, Martin, & Bender, 2002). Given the problems with attrition and mobility, the demand for new teachers in special education annually is greater than in general education (Boe, 2006; Boe, Bobbitt, & Cook, 1997; Boe, Bobbit, & Cook, 1998; Boe, Bobbitt, Cook, Whitener, & Weber, 1997; Whitaker, 2000). Given the financial cost of teacher replacement to the school district and taxpayers, the reasons for the attrition rate as well as potential methods for reducing attrition and mobility must be investigated.

Researchers have identified several primary reasons for the high rates of attrition seen among special education teachers (Fore et al., 2002; Gehrke & Murri, 2006; Schlichte, Yssel, & Merbler, 2005; Thornton, Peltier, & Medina, 2007; Whitaker, 2003; White & Mason, 2006). Undesirable working conditions contribute to attrition and include such factors as heavy class loads/caseloads, job stress, burdensome paperwork, lack of planning time, insufficient materials, job assignments (multiple responsibilities), and an unsupportive school climate. Student issues also affect special education teachers and contribute to attrition and include such factors as extreme diversity, types of disabilities, discipline problems, low motivation, and lack of student progress. Lack of support adds to the rate of attrition and includes such concerns as a lack of teacher peer support, insufficient administrator support, lack of parental support, and insufficient provision of professional development and understanding of the general curriculum. Additionally, personal and employment conditions such as reductions in force contribute to the rate of attrition.

In addition to the factors described above, special education teachers are faced with the difficult and sometimes discouraging task of educating students with severe disabilities. A study of over 650 special education teachers revealed that the highest burnout area in special education includes working with students exhibiting emotional and behavior disabilities (Singh & Billingsley, 1996). The survey showed that teachers who work with students with these disabilities were less likely to stay in special education when compared to teachers who primarily worked with students of varying other disabilities. Programming options available to students as well as the responsibilities associated with facilitating inclusion of disabled students are often reported as reasons for leaving the field (Gehrke & Murri, 2006). Gehrke and Murri found that being responsible for the supervision of paraprofessionals was another factor contributing to the frustrations of special educators. Brownell, Smith, McNellis, and Miller (1997) found that most of the special educators who left took positions in other areas of education. These teachers were characterized as disgruntled because of the sense of being unprepared and overwhelmed. The stress of being unsupported coupled with high student needs leads to a sense of being disempowered. Those who were considered nondisgruntled left for reasons such as pay, certification problems, family reasons, or positions being eliminated. Whitaker (2003) indicated that special education teachers need the most assistance with system information, such as policies and procedures, and that emotional support was the next most-needed area of assistance. This study identified that the amount of assistance needed (as identified by self-report) was discrepant from the amount of assistance received in all areas where assistance was provided.

The case for mentoring and induction of special education teachers is made stronger in light of the aforementioned problems with teacher retention and costs associated with the replacement of teachers. Fortunately, the research literature demonstrates benefits for special educators who are mentored (Boyer & Gillespie, 2000; Kennedy & Burnstein, 2004; Schlichte et al., 2005; Thornton et al., 2007;

Whitaker, 2000a; Whitaker, 2000b; White & Mason, 2006). Mentoring for first-year special education teachers alleviates feelings of isolation, as mentors not only assist with instructional support and paperwork but also provide encouragement and compassion. In Schlichte and colleagues' (2005) study, teachers who were interviewed attributed success in their first year to mentoring, collegial relationships, and a sense of belonging to the school. Whitaker (2000a) analyzed self-report data from 156 first-year special education teachers and found that the perceived effectiveness of mentor programs increased with weekly mentor/protégé contact and that unstructured/informal (spontaneous) meetings were more effective than formal (facilitated) mentoring sessions. Further, for those teachers who rated mentors as effective, common characteristics were identified. Mentors and protégés met frequently, mentors provided emotional support, systems information was related to teaching in special education, and information about materials and resources was shared. The single most important characteristic was that mentors also were special educators. Additional studies support the contention that mentors and protégés in special education should be well-matched. Whitaker (2003) found that new special education teachers received significantly larger amounts of assistance from other special educators compared to administrators or mentors who were not special education teachers. As cited in White and Mason (2006), Griffin and colleagues found that frequent contact, mentors matched based on special education background, and nonevaluative roles of mentors led to the most effective mentoring programs.

Thornton et al. (2007) suggests that mentor programs should be mandatory for first-year special education teachers because these programs help strengthen teacher performance and reduce the likelihood of attrition. Mentor programs capitalize on existing resources (e.g., the experience and knowledge of the mentor), are cost effective, and increase teacher satisfaction and school performance. Although benefits have been demonstrated for mentoring special education teachers, not all of the literature clearly supports the efforts of induction and mentoring. For example, Billingsley (2004) found that although there were benefits to induction, neither induction support nor mentoring was highly correlated with teachers' intentions to continue teaching in special education. Although this was the only published study demonstrating a lack of significant relationship between mentoring and positive outcomes, it is possible that additional studies with null results remain unpublished and, therefore, are not reviewed here.

Connections to Satisfaction, Commitment, and Stress

Commitment and job satisfaction have been studied primarily in the business and organizational fields for a number of reasons. Research indicates that people who are committed to an organization are more likely to work toward organizational goals and remain with the organization and are likely to report higher levels of job satisfaction (Billingsley, 1992; Egan & Song, 2008; Kammeyer-Mueller & Judge, 2008; Lankau et al., 2006; Seibert, 1999; Waters, 2004). These studies imply that cost is always involved when there is employee turnover, and an increase in commitment may lead to higher effort on the job, both of which make commitment highly desirable by employers. In their pioneering work on organizational commitment, Mowday, Porter, and Steers (1982) proposed that committed individuals are more likely to work effectively toward meeting organizational goals and stay with the organization, and when individuals are not as committed, they have higher intentions of quitting. Defining commitment and satisfaction are important to the study of their effects on employee retention, and retention of teachers for this study specifically.

Both organizational commitment and job satisfaction are conceptualizations of one's job attitude. Organizational commitment can be defined as "attitudinal" or "behavioral," as cited in Billingsley (1992). Attitudinal commitment is based on three factors: belief in and acceptance of organizational goals and values; a strong willingness on the part of the employee to put much effort into the organization's goals; and a strong desire by the employee to remain with the organization. The behavioral definition indicates that commitment is a function of the costs (e.g., time, frustration) and rewards (e.g., money, sense of purpose) associated with being a member of the organization. Similarly, Egan and Song (2008) defined commitment as a psychological bond that binds an employee to the organization. The person-organization fit implies congruence between the employee and the organization and its goals. Job satisfaction is commonly defined as the affective reaction of an employee, whereas commitment is often considered a behavioral reaction (Billingsley, 1992; Egan & Song, 2008). Although research is unclear as to whether satisfaction precedes commitment or vice versa (Billingsley & Cross, 1992) or whether there is a causal connection between the two, there is an unquestionably strong connection between commitment and satisfaction, and some argue that job satisfaction causes organizational commitment.

Research outside the realm of education supports the notion that both job satisfaction and organizational commitment are affected by mentoring and induction. In their meta-analysis, Allen et al. (2004) found a positive relationship between mentoring relationships and job satisfaction. Mentored individuals were more satisfied with and committed to their career than nonmentored individuals. In addition, both career and psychosocial mentoring functions were positively related to satisfaction. Overall, Allen et al. found that affective reactions and psychological feelings were more consistent benefits of mentoring compared to more objective career success indicators such as compensation and promotion. Other than the Allen et al. meta-analysis, Egan and Song (2008) reported that little systematic research has been conducted examining mentoring and its effect on satisfaction and commitment. Egan and Song conducted the first known randomized experimental comparison study in this area and found that those employees participating in high-level facilitated (i.e., formal) mentoring showed the highest levels of job satisfaction and organizational commitment when compared to the low-level facilitated mentoring groups. Both high- and low-facilitated mentoring groups demonstrated stronger scores on measures of satisfaction, organizational commitment, and person-organization fit when compared to the nonmentored control group. In addition to these results, the mentored groups also demonstrated stronger manager performance ratings when compared to the nonmentored group. Research conducted by Waters (2004) found that protégé-mentor agreement was significantly related to both job satisfaction and organizational commitment. In addition, perceptions of received support by the protégé correlated highly with feelings of satisfaction. These findings have potential implications for mentoring within the schools and the importance of matching mentors and protégés.

Studies have found that, in general, teachers as an occupational group report higher levels of satisfaction when compared to other occupational groups (Borg & Riding, 1991). Although research in education has not been as systematic and controlled as in other fields, some studies have reported the effects of mentoring on job satisfaction and organizational commitment. Whitaker (2000a) found a positive correlation between mentoring effectiveness and protégés' job satisfaction and retention. In her review, Whitaker (2000b) indicated that teachers who participate in induction/mentoring programs are more satisfied and committed to their jobs and are less likely to leave the profession. Cooley and Yovanoff (1996) found that participants in treatment groups who participated in stress-management and peer-collaboration workshops showed higher levels of job satisfaction and organizational commitment compared to control groups. Although not formal mentoring, such intervention could impact the delivery of induction and mentoring programs. Similarly, Billingsley (1992) found that commitment was a significant predictor of both general and special education teachers' intentions to stay in education. Job satisfaction was found to be influenced by leadership support, work involvement, reduced role conflict, and reduced levels of stress. In a more recent study, more than

60% of special education teachers beginning their career reported having mentoring available to them. Among those respondents who found mentoring helpful, most indicated that informal assistance from their colleagues was more beneficial than the formal mentoring programs (Billingsley, Carlson, & Klein, 2004). Additionally, this study found that those who reported assistance to be helpful identified their jobs as more manageable than those who did not report induction support to be helpful. Contrary to Whitaker's (2000a) findings, Billingsley et al. found that the helpfulness of induction support was not significantly correlated to teachers' intention to maintain a career in special education.

The effect of work-related stress on job satisfaction and organizational commitment has been studied to some extent. Stress has been defined in education as a teacher experiencing "unpleasant, negative emotions, such as anger, anxiety, tension, frustration or depression, resulting from some aspect of their work as a teacher" (Kyriacou, 2001, p. 28). Feelings such as frustration, tension, and anxiety were indications of work-related stress that were identified through Strong's (2005) review of the literature (Kyriacou, 1987; Kyriacou, 2001). From these reviews, identified sources of teacher stress have included teaching unmotivated students, difficulty maintaining discipline, heavy workloads, limited time, and role conflict and ambiguity, to name a few. Early research has identified role conflict and role ambiguity as dimensions of stress that are predictive of job dissatisfaction (Rizzo, House, & Lirtzman, 1970). Role conflict is the phenomenon that occurs when information given to an employee about roles and responsibilities conflicts with the realities of the employee's daily duties and responsibilities, and role ambiguity refers to the feeling an employee has when he or she has been provided with insufficient information to perform roles and responsibilities adequately (Wisniewski & Gargiulo, 1997). Gersten and colleagues (2001) used the term *role dissonance* to refer to these concepts and found that educators who perceive dissonance between job expectations and actual requirements were more stressed and less satisfied with their position compared to those who did not perceive dissonance. They concluded that stress plays a mediating role in influencing a teacher's decision to leave education and special education in particular.

In his review of the literature, Strong (2005) concluded that negative working conditions, particularly stress, have an effect on attrition. Billingsley (1993) reported that higher rates of attrition in special education are often attributed to stress due to working with certain populations within special education. Thus far, mixed results have been found in terms of comparisons of stress between general and special educators, with some studies identifying more stress with general educators, some studies identifying more stress with special educators, and some studies finding no difference between the groups. In addition, several studies have found attrition to be at least partially attributed to stress (Billingsley & Cross, 1991; Billingsley & Cross, 1992; Lauritzen, 1986; McKnab, 1983; Platt & Olsen, 1990, Seery, 1990). Borg and Riding (1991) argued that significant levels of stress could be reasonably expected to contribute to a teacher's performance and thus impact the education of children. These authors found that the majority of the 545 teachers surveyed found their work to be satisfying, and those that reported satisfaction were more likely to report that they would choose teaching as a career again if given the chance. Those teachers who reported higher levels of stress also reported lower job satisfaction.

In the human resource literature, Lankau et al. (2006) identified role conflict and role ambiguity as two types of work stress that influence job satisfaction, commitment, and retention. Lankau et al. found that functions of mentoring such as role modeling and vocational support reduced role conflict and role ambiguity. In turn, perceptions of job satisfaction and organizational commitment were associated with reductions in role conflict and role ambiguity. In contrast, Seibert (1999) found that facilitated mentoring did not affect a protégé's work-role stress or self-esteem at work. However, although not statistically significant, Seibert did find that psychosocial mentoring was related to reports of lower work-role stress. While much of the literature has touted the importance of mentoring programs for general and special education teachers alike, no systematic, quantitative study has been found that explicitly examines work-related stress and the impact of mentoring on protégé stress.

Lankau et al. (2006) identified in their sample of business management graduates that increased psychosocial support through mentoring was associated with fewer stressors. Specifically, Lankau et al. identified that role ambiguity and role conflict served as significant mediators in the relationship between psychosocial support and job attitudes (as measured by satisfaction and commitment) as well as role modeling and job attitude. Lower perceptions of role conflict and role ambiguity were connected with the role modeling aspect of mentoring, and lower perceptions of role conflict were connected to the vocational support aspect of mentoring. The goal of the current study is to identify whether the work-related stressors of role conflict and role ambiguity mediate the relationship between mentoring functions and job attitude (as measured by job satisfaction and organizational commitment). As suggested by Lankau et al., mentoring functions are hypothesized to lead to improved job attitude by reducing stress.

Summary of the Literature

Mentoring has been identified as an effective mechanism for guiding new employees as they venture into their career paths as well as for helping these employees adapt to and learn the cultures of their new employing organization. Mentoring has also been established as a way to retain professionals in the field in general, and in the field of education in particular (Ingersoll & Kralik, 2004; Smith & Ingersoll, 2004). First-year teachers struggle with such responsibilities as managing time, motivating students, managing students' behavior, differentiating instruction, and communicating with parents and school personnel (Gehrke & Murri, 2006; Melnick & Meister, 2008). The current review of the literature identified that mentoring not only helps first-year teachers with the aforementioned struggles but may also result in lower attrition of teachers within their first five years, improved instruction, increased potential for improved student achievement, increased job satisfaction, increased levels of organizational commitment, and lower levels of work-related stress.

The literature also offers several components that compose a quality mentoring program. Perhaps most importantly, specific functions of mentoring have been identified which are believed to lead to more positive levels of job attitude and retention in the field. Career support, psychosocial support, and role modeling have been identified as distinct and critical functions of mentoring which have been positively related to organizational outcomes such as job satisfaction and organizational commitment (Allen et al., 2004; Egan & Song, 2008; Lankau et al., 2006). The results of such studies have supported the notion that mentoring is an effective intervention for first-year employees. This suggests the continued need for quality mentoring programs with qualified mentors who understand the importance of covering functions of mentoring in their role as mentor.

The role of stress on first-year employees, including first-year general education and special education teachers, has also been reviewed in the literature. Role conflict and role ambiguity are established dimensions of stress which have been demonstrated to negatively predict job satisfaction and organizational commitment (Gersten et al., 2001; Rizzo, House, & Lirtzman, 1970), and teacher attrition has been found to be at least partially attributable to stress (Billingsley & Cross, 1991; Billingsley & Cross, 1992; Lauritzen, 1986; McKnab, 1983; Platt & Olsen, 1990, Seery, 1990). Lankau et al. (2006) have identified that the three functions of mentoring can reduce stress. In a sample of business professionals, these researchers found stress to be a mediating factor in the fulfillment of mentoring functions positively predicting job satisfaction and organizational commitment. Given the research base on teacher attrition, the positive effect of mentoring on measures of job

attitude that predict teacher attrition, and the effect of stress and burnout on teacher

retention, identifying the nature of the role of stress on teachers' job attitudes and how

this is affected by the fulfillment of mentoring functions is critical. These findings

may have implications for the types of mentoring activities that should occur within an

established mentoring program as well as the importance of identifying stress-

reducing mechanisms or strategies aimed at assisting first-year teachers.

CHAPTER 3

METHODOLOGY

This chapter outlines the research approach and design which were utilized to

answer the research questions and hypotheses regarding the effects of mentoring on

job attitude. The study proposes that reductions in work-related stress, as measured by

role conflict and role ambiguity, mediate the positive relationship between mentoring

and protégés' attitudes. As previously described through the review of the literature,

role conflict and role ambiguity have been found to decrease job satisfaction,

organizational commitment, and intention to remain in a job. This study sought to

identify if these role stressors mediate the relationships between the mentoring

functions (i.e., career support, psychosocial support, and role modeling) and job

satisfaction and organizational commitment, both of which are well-established

outcomes of mentoring. Additionally, analyses were conducted to determine if there

was a significant difference in the mediating effects of stress on outcomes of job

attitude between general education teachers and special education teachers. In order to

answer the proposed questions, a quantitative research method was utilized.

Quantitative methods answer questions by quantifying data into numerical form and

then statistically analyzing this data. Gall, Gall, and Borg (2007) define quantitative

research as "inquiry that is grounded in the assumption that features of the social environment constitute an objective reality that is relatively constant across time and settings" (p. 650).

The study was guided by the expectation that higher levels of the mentoring functions of career support, psychosocial support, and role modeling are associated with lower levels of role stressors among protégés and that lower levels of role stressors are associated with a more positive job attitude (i.e., higher levels of job satisfaction and organizational commitment). It was hypothesized that the positive relationships between the mentoring functions and job attitude would weaken once the effects of the role stressors were taken into account. Whether the strength or nature of the relationships between the mentoring functions, role stressors, and job attitude differ between special education or regular education teachers was also analyzed.

In order to answer the research questions and hypotheses, teachers with two to ten years of teaching experience were targeted for participation in the survey. The survey asked questions about the mentoring program each teacher was involved in during his/her first year of teaching and also included specific questions about the type and amount of mentoring received. Finally, participants were asked to complete attitude surveys. Participants included general education and special education teachers.

Population and Sample

Participants consisted of teachers who, at the time of their participation, were employed by small, medium, or large suburban school districts in northern Illinois.

Five thousand five hundred thirty-five teachers from districts with formal mentoring programs were recruited for volunteer participation through convenience sampling which included contacting suburban districts with principals or other administrators known professionally, both directly and indirectly, by the researcher. Participants also were recruited through identification on district websites. Teachers were recruited from public school elementary districts, high school districts, and unit (K-12) school districts that had a mentoring program in place for first-year teachers. Participating teachers were sought from any grade level and, therefore, were employed at a variety of grade level centers (e.g., preschool, elementary, middle school, or high school). Participants in the study were delimited to those within their second to tenth year of teaching in their current employing district. Only general education and special education teachers were recruited for participation; related service providers or pupil services personnel were specifically not recruited and therefore excluded. First-year teachers also were excluded from the recruitment and analyses because at the time of the research they were still directly involved in the mentoring process. Teachers in their second to tenth years were targeted, as they were expected to have a higher likelihood of having participated in a mentoring program and to have a greater recollection of their experiences in that mentoring program compared to those teaching beyond ten years. Some teachers with more than ten years of teaching experience in the current employing district were inadvertently included in the request for participation; however, only general education and special education teachers meeting the specified criteria were included in the data analyses.

In order to assess whether participants were involved in a mentoring relationship, a mentor was defined as "an individual (typically a more senior member of your organization) who has advanced experience and knowledge and who is committed to the enhancement and support of your career" (Kram, 1985). All participants who indicated that they had no mentoring at the start of their career within their current employing district were excluded from the data analyses.

Selection of Participants

Participants were selected using a convenience sampling technique. The researcher contacted principals and district administrators from multiple schools in northern Illinois and requested access to contact information for employees in their district/school who met the specifications for participation. Seniority reports were specifically requested from these districts. Through the seniority reports, teachers in their second to tenth year of teaching in a district were identified. The researcher communicated with the identified district or school contact person in order to ensure the acquisition of appropriate participants based on the selection criteria. For some districts, staff listings were identified from district websites, and teachers were identified from lists made publicly available on these websites. Email addresses were collected and distribution of research materials (e.g., letter of consent, questionnaires, and surveys) took place electronically. In total, teachers from eleven districts were included in the recruitment process. Of the eleven districts represented in the sample, eight were unit school districts and three were elementary districts. Seniority lists were made available from seven of the districts, while potential participants were identified from public websites from four of the districts.

Participants and Sample Size

Of the 5,535 recruited teachers, 339 individuals (6%) began participating in the survey. Of the 293 teachers who completed the survey, 260 (88.7%) were identified as having met the specified criteria for participation in the study. The final sample included 216 (83.0%) female and 44 (17.0%) male teachers.

Protection of Human Subjects

Confidentiality was strictly maintained. Individual teacher names and employing schools were not and will at no time be made public or used in written documents. A letter of consent explaining the volunteer nature of participation was provided electronically to each participant. Since information was confidential, there was no threat to individual teacher reputation or employment in the district. Additionally, the letter of consent explained that participation would pose no risk of injury or need for medical treatment. Electronic completion and submission of the research materials and individual consent form signified and acknowledged consent for participation.

Instrumentation and Data Collection

The data collection method utilized in this study was survey research. Specifically, self-report questionnaires were utilized with the selected sample that represented the population (e.g., general and special education teachers) being studied and by which results were generalized (Gall et al., 2007). Surveys are useful tools because they enable researchers to collect data from a large number of people and to examine relationships between variables that would be less feasible using an experimental design (e.g., because random assignments to groups is not possible).

Data collection began with communication to the studied districts' administrative authorities, principals, and/or the Mentoring and Induction Coordinator. After receiving verbal confirmation that the school and/or district administrator(s) would assist with teacher identification for participation in the study, recruitment letters were emailed to potential participants (see Appendix A). For districts with no personal administrative contacts, district websites were utilized to retrieve potential participant email addresses, and recruitment letters were emailed to these potential participants. The letter described the nature of the study, how aggregated results would be communicated back to participants, and the confidential nature of participant responses. The questionnaires were accessible via the Internet through a link provided in the emailed recruitment letter. At the start of the electronic survey, information was provided formalizing the agreement between the researcher and the individual respondents which outlined the process for participation and survey completion as well as explained their consent for participation by continuation in the survey.

Assurances of confidentiality were communicated once again (see Appendix B). Each participant was asked to complete a demographics page, an induction/mentoring support questionnaire, a mentoring functions questionnaire, and measures of psychosocial outcomes including those measuring job satisfaction, organizational commitment, and work-related stress (see Appendix C).

Approximately two to four weeks following the initial recruitment contact, a follow-up recruitment letter was emailed to potential participants reminding them of the request for participation. Several weeks after the initial recruitment letter, a third contact via email was made to those participants who had not yet responded to the recruitment letter. These follow-up letters included the same recruitment information as the initial contact (see Appendix D and Appendix E).

In order to demonstrate appreciation for their volunteered time, participants were eligible to receive one of 10 $25 Visa gift cards. Upon completion of data collection, all participants who agreed to participate through completion of the electronic consent form (regardless of their ultimate completion of the survey and regardless of whether they met the specified criteria for inclusion in the study) were entered into a drawing where they had an equal chance of being selected to receive one of the ten gift cards. The ten winners were notified directly by the researcher.

Survey feasibility was obtained by a pilot study procedure where approximately eight teachers were asked to complete the survey for review and feedback. These pilot study respondents were contacted via email following their completion of the survey. Through a series of questions, they were asked to critique the format, clarity, and user-friendliness of the questionnaires. Respondents also were asked to provide feedback on the ease of electronic submission and understandability of the directions. Participants in the pilot study were encouraged to contact the researcher by phone or email if additional information or clarification of responses was needed, and in some cases the individuals were contacted directly by the researcher to ask follow-up questions. Pilot study data indicated that the survey was completed with ease and all components were clear to the participants.

Measures

A multi-page electronic questionnaire was administered to participants in order to measure demographic information, perceived induction/mentoring support, level of perceived support received by mentoring function, work-related stress, job satisfaction, and organizational commitment. The questionnaire was developed by modifying or using the extant instruments for each outcome area measured.

Personal Demographics

The survey research for this study asked that each participant report on his/her: (a) primary teaching position (teacher type), (b) gender, (c) number of total years teaching, d) number of years teaching with their current district (e.g., counting the current year of teaching as one year), (e) tenure process status, (f) school type, and (g) school size. Respondents also were asked questions about their mentors as well as the level of mentoring received in their current positions, including: (a) whether they are or were involved in a mentoring program, (b) years involved in the mentoring program, (c) range of formal/facilitated mentoring/induction sessions participated in, (d) range of informal/spontaneous one-on-one mentoring sessions participated in, (e) the primary teaching position of the mentor, and (f) whether the mentor was located in the same building.

Total Mentoring/Induction Support

Total mentoring and induction support was assessed using a measure developed by Quinn and Andrews (2004). The twenty-item questionnaire is based on research addressing areas crucial to supporting the needs of novice teachers. Crucial areas include: (a) assistance with instruction, (b) personal and emotional support, (c) access to resources, (d) information about policies and procedures, (e) assistance with management and discipline, and (f) support with parent interaction. Respondents were asked to rate each of the twenty items on a six-point scale (1 = very strongly disagree to 6 = very strongly agree). Responses were added together and divided by the number of items to determine a mean score for level of perceived support. Strong internal consistency (Cronbach's Alpha = .94) was demonstrated in the current sample.

Mentoring Functions

The amount of mentoring support received by each mentoring function was measured using an abbreviated version of the Mentoring Functions Questionnaire

(MFQ; Scandura, 1992). Following a validation study of the original 15-item MFQ (Castro, Scandura, & Williams, 2006), the questionnaire was reduced to nine items (MFQ-9). The MFQ-9 consists of three three-item subscales, each representing one of the three mentoring functions (i.e., vocational/career, psychosocial, role modeling). All items were rated on a six-point scale with 1 indicating "very strongly disagree" and 6 indicating "very strongly agree." Responses from each subscale were added together and divided by the number of items (3) to determine a mean score for level of perceived support. Based on the Castro et al. study, the internal consistency estimate for the MFQ-9 total score was .78, and the reliability coefficients for each of the three subscales (career/vocational, psychosocial, and role modeling) were .67, .77, and .69, respectively. The reliability coefficient (i.e., Cronbach's Alpha) was .94 for each of the three subscales (career, psychosocial, role modeling) in the current sample.

Work-Related Stress

Work-related stress was assessed through a role conflict and ambiguity scale. A total of 14 items comprise the scale developed by Rizzo, House, and Lirtzman (1970), which measures the degree of role stress a person may experience in their work. The role conflict scale is composed of eight items and alpha coefficients have been reported from .70 to .87 (Fields, 2004; Lankau et al., 2006). The role ambiguity scale is composed of six items, and alpha coefficients for this scale have been reported from .71 to .95 (Fields; Lankau et al.). Respondents rated the questionnaire items on a six-point scale (1 = very strongly disagree to 6 = very strongly agree). Role conflict and role ambiguity were computed as the average of the items for each scale, with high scores reflecting greater role conflict and role ambiguity. Cronbach's Alpha for the current sample on the conflict scale was .85, and the Cronbach's Alpha on the role ambiguity scale was .88.

Job Satisfaction

The job satisfaction subscale (three items) from the Michigan Organizational Assessment Questionnaire (MOAQ; Cammann, Fichman, Jenkins, & Klesh, 1979, 1983) was used to measure overall job satisfaction. Respondents rated the questionnaire items on a six-point scale (1 = very strongly disagree to 6 = very strongly agree). In their meta-analysis, Bowling and Hammond (2008) concluded that the job satisfaction subscale of the MOAQ is a reliable and construct-valid measure of job satisfaction and suggested its use for assessing global job satisfaction. A score for each individual was derived from the average of responses to each of the three items in the subscale. Previous studies have shown Cronbach's Alpha coefficients for this measure ranging from .77 to .90 (Egan & Song, 2008; Spector, 1985; Lankau et al., 2006), and Fields (2002) cited reliability coefficient values ranging from .67 to .95 from a variety of studies completed in the 1990s. Cronbach's Alpha for the current study sample was .91.

Organizational Commitment

Organizational commitment was measured utilizing a modified version of the Organizational Commitment Questionnaire (OCQ; Porter & Smith, 1970; Porter, Steers, Mowday, & Boulian, 1974). The shortened nine-item OCQ measures employee commitment to an organization and has demonstrated a large positive correlation with the 15-item OCQ (Fields, 2004). Respondents rated their agreement to each item on a six-point scale (1 = very strongly disagree to 6 = very strongly agree). Items were averaged to form a single score for each participant. High scores indicate stronger organizational commitment, which is defined as an affective attachment that is characterized by loyalty to the organization, acceptance of organizational values, a desire to remain with the organization, and a willingness to exert effort on behalf of the organization. Alpha coefficients for the OCQ have ranged from .74 to .92 (Fields, 2004; Lankau et al., 2006; Lam, 1998; Seibert1999). Test-retest reliability has been found to be moderate (Lam, 1998). Cronbach's Alpha for the current study's sample was .93.

Data Analysis

To examine the bivariate relationships between the variables of interest, Pearson correlation coefficients were calculated between the measures of mentoring functions (i.e., career support, psychosocial support, role modeling), role stressors (i.e., role conflict, role ambiguity) and job attitude (i.e., job satisfaction, organizational commitment) using PASW 17.0 (IBM Corp., Somers, NY).

To test whether role stressors mediated the relationship between the mentoring functions and job attitude, structural equation modeling (SEM) was conducted using AMOS 17.0 (Amos Development Corp., Crawfordville, FL) , which generates full information maximum likelihood parameter estimates even in the presence of missing data. Indicators for each latent construct in the model were created using the item parcel technique outlined by Floyd and Widaman (1995, as cited in Lankau et al., 2006). Specifically, items were randomly assigned to item parcels and the items for each parcel were averaged. Scales with eight or less items had two parcels and scales with more than eight items had three parcels. The use of item parcels is preferable to the use of individual items as indicators in order to maintain an adequate sample size to parameter ratio (Lankau et al., 2006). However, because the MFQ-9 subscales and the measure of job satisfaction had only three items each, individual items were used as indicators for the latent constructs of career support, psychosocial support, role modeling, and job satisfaction. Several goodness of fit indices were used to evaluate model fit, including chi-square, comparative fit index (CFI), Tucker-Lewis Index (TLI), and root mean square error of approximation (RMSEA). Ideally, chi-square results will be nonsignificant, CFI and TLI will be greater than .95, and RMSEA will be less than .06 (Hu & Bentler, 1999).

All other analyses (i.e., chi square, correlation, Analyses of Variance [ANOVA]) were conducted using PASW 17.0 (IBM Corp., Somers, NY). Role modeling (-3.96) and job satisfaction (-3.10) scores demonstrated significant negative skew. Attempts to transform the data using log- and square root-transformations did not improve the normality of the distribution; however, the distributions of the data appeared reasonable. Consequently, the original variables were used in all analyses.

Figure 1 displays the original hypothesized mediational relationships between the specified measures. This examination of relationships between variables is based on a model utilized by Lankau et al. (2006) which studied similar outcomes using a sample of professionals who had graduated from universities with degrees in business management within the previous 20 years.

Multigroup SEM was employed to examine potential differences in the model for special education versus general education teachers. Potential differences in demographic variables (i.e., gender, number of years teaching, etc.) were examined among the special education vs. general education teachers using nonparametric (i.e., chi-square) analyses for the categorical variables (i.e., gender, number of completed years teaching in district, tenure process status, school type, school size, range of formal/facilitated mentoring sessions, range of informal/spontaneous one-one mentoring sessions) and an ANOVA for the continuous variable total number of years teaching.

Seven-Factor Mediational Model

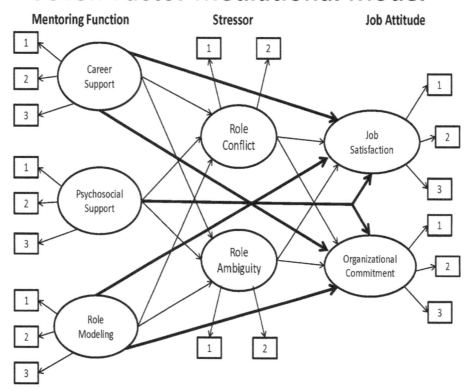

Figure 1.   Hypothesized seven-factor model.

Note: Each outer box is an indicator of its associated latent construct.

CHAPTER 4

RESULTS

Of the 260 participants, 159 (61%) identified themselves as tenured teachers

and 98 (38%) identified themselves as probationary (nontenured), while three

participants (1%) failed to report their tenure status (see Table 1). The majority (87%)

of participants were from unit (k-12) districts, 34 (13%) of the participants were from

elementary districts, and none of the participants were from high school districts. One

hundred eleven participants (43%) reported working in elementary schools, 74 (28%)

reported working in middle schools, and 75 (29%) reported working in high schools

(see Table 2). General education teachers comprised the majority ($n = 206$, 79%) of

the sample and the remaining 54 (21%) were special education teachers.

The bivariate correlations between each of the mentor function variables (i.e.,

career support, psychosocial support, and role modeling), work-related stress variables

(i.e., role conflict and role ambiguity) and psychosocial outcome variables (i.e., job

satisfaction and organizational commitment) are listed in Table 3. As expected, most

of the mentor function variables were significantly negatively correlated with both role

Table 1

Frequency Counts and Percentages of Study Demographic Variables

Variable	n	Percent (%)
Gender ($N = 260$)		
Female	216	83.1
Male	44	16.9
Primary Teaching Position ($N = 260$)		
General Education	206	79.2
Special Education	54	20.8
Tenure Status ($N = 257$)		
Tenured	159	61.9
Probationary	98	38.1
Type of School ($N = 260$)		
Elementary School	111	42.7
Middle School	74	28.5
High School	75	28.8
Type of District ($N = 259$)		
Unit K-12	225	86.9
Elementary	34	13.1
High School	0	0
Student Population of School ($N = 258$)		
0-199	8	3.1
200-499	58	22.5
500-799	65	25.2
800-1199	56	21.7
1200+	71	27.5
Total Years Teaching ($N = 260$)		
2-5	95	36.5
6-10	121	46.4
11-15	26	10.0
16-20	9	3.6
21+	9	3.5
Total Years Teaching in Current District ($N = 260$)		
2	27	10.4
3	31	11.9
4	35	13.5
5	42	16.2
6	28	10.8
7	26	10.0
8	20	7.7
9	16	6.2
10	35	13.5

Table 2

Characteristics of Participants' Mentoring Experiences

Variable	*n*	Percent (%)
Required to participate in a mentoring program when in current employing district ($N = 260$)		
Yes	249	95.8
No	11	4.2
Mentoring consisted of participation in formal meetings ($N = 258$)		
Yes	219	84.9
No	39	15.1
Mentoring consisted of participation in informal meetings/1:1 sessions with mentor ($N = 257$)		
Yes	224	87.2
No	33	12.8
The assigned mentor taught in a similar position as mentee in the first year ($N = 259$)		
Yes	205	79.2
No	54	20.8
Type of District ($N = 259$)		
Unit K-12	225	86.8
Elementary	34	13.1
High School	0	0
The assigned mentor taught in the same school as mentee in the first year ($N = 260$)		
Yes	219	84.2
No	41	15.8
Length of mentoring program in current district ($N = 260$)		
1 Year	116	44.6
2 Years	139	53.5
2+ Years	5	1.9
Mentoring was a valuable part of mentee's early career development ($N = 260$)		
Agree	173	66.5
Disagree	87	33.5

Table 3

Correlations, Means, and Standard Deviations of Study Variables

Variable	1	2	3	4	5	6	7
1. Vocational support							
2. Psychosocial support	.82***						
3. Role modeling	.82***	.81***					
4. Role conflict	-.15*	-.03	-.16*				
5. Role ambiguity	-.23***	-.15*	-.22***	.56***			
6. Job satisfaction	.27***	.21***	.23***	-.48***	-.52***		
7. Organizational commitment	.33***	.25***	.33***	-.35***	-.47***	.71***	
M	3.98	3.82	4.01	3.54	2.88	4.78	4.49
SD	1.30	1.38	1.30	.79	.79	.95	.88

Note. Pairwise *N*s vary from 228 to 249.

* $p < .05$. ** $p < .01$. *** $p < .001$.

conflict and role ambiguity, suggesting that increased support from one's mentor was associated with less work-related stress (however, psychosocial support was not significantly related to role conflict). Likewise, each of the mentor function variables was significantly positively associated with both psychosocial outcome variables, indicating that increased support from one's mentor was associated with increased job satisfaction and organizational commitment. Finally, both work-related stress variables were significantly negatively associated with the psychosocial outcome variables, indicating that higher scores on role conflict and ambiguity were associated with lower scores on job satisfaction and organizational commitment (see Table 3).

Predicting Job Satisfaction and Organizational Commitment

Because latent variables are not directly measured or observed they must be inferred by their associated indicators. The extent to which the observed indicators are related to their underlying latent variables is referred to as the measurement model. Therefore, as recommended by Anderson and Gerbing's (1988) two-step method, the first step in conducting SEM was to assess the fit of the measurement model using confirmatory factor analysis (CFA).

In the current study, the measurement model was first fitted as a model consisting of seven latent variables (i.e., career support, psychosocial support, role modeling, role conflict, role ambiguity, job satisfaction, and organizational commitment; see Figure 1). All of the predicted factor loadings were positive and highly significant ($ps < .001$), which signified that the indicators were representative of their associated latent constructs. However, when the chi-square value and goodness of fit indices were examined, the seven-factor measurement model demonstrated poor fit, $\chi^2 (131) = 327.94$, $p < .001$, comparative fit index (CFI) = .96, Tucker-Lewis Index (TLI) = .94, root mean square error of approximation (RMSEA) = .08. Modification indices were examined to determine where the problems in fit lay within the model. Seventeen of the 43 identified modifications that could improve model fit (not all of which should be considered because they are not theoretically grounded) suggested that indicators of one mentor function also should load on another mentor function variable. These identified cross-loadings suggest that the three mentor function variables are not as distinct as the seven-factor model implies. This finding is consistent with the high correlations among the variables ($rs > .80$, see Table 3), suggesting the likelihood of a single latent variable encompassing all three of the mentor function variables. Because multicollinearity (i.e., high correlations) among the predictors can lead to instability in the analyses (Kline, 1998), the measurement model was revised such that career support, psychosocial support, and role modeling composite scores were specified as indicators of the latent variable mentor function.

A second CFA was conducted to test a five-factor measurement model, in which mentor function was indicated by career support, psychosocial support, and role modeling and the remaining latent factors were unchanged. The five-factor measurement model also demonstrated relatively poor fit, $\chi^2 (55) = 134.05$, $p < .001$, CFI = .97, TLI = .95, RMSEA = .07. Modification indices suggested that items on the organizational commitment factor also loaded on the job satisfaction factor, suggesting

that these two variables could be combined into a single latent variable. Again, this

modification was consistent with the high correlation ($r = .71$, see Table 3) between

job satisfaction and organizational commitment. A final CFA was conducted to test a

four-factor measurement model that consisted of mentor function, role conflict, role

ambiguity, and job attitude (indicated by job satisfaction and organizational

commitment). As was true in both the seven- and five-factor measurement models, all

predicted loadings were positive and highly significant in the four-factor model. In

addition, the four-factor model demonstrated good fit, χ^2 (21) = 41.63, $p = .01$, CFI =

.99, TLI = .97, RMSEA = .06. Because the four-factor measurement model

demonstrated the best fit, the structural model was tested on the four-factor model (see

Figure 2). (Note. The structural model also was tested on the seven- and five-factor

models and the results for these analyses are presented in Appendix F.)

To establish mediation, it is necessary to first establish the presence of three

sets of associations: a relationship between Mentor Functions and the proposed

mediators (role conflict, role ambiguity), a relationship between Mentor Functions and

the proposed outcome of interest (Job Attitude), and a relationship between the

proposed mediator and proposed outcome. As seen in Table 3, the sets of associations

(i.e., significant correlations) between all of these variables were established. The

next step was to examine the structural model to test whether the relationship between

Mentor Functions and Job Attitude was mediated by role conflict and role ambiguity

(see Figure 2). Because scale scores were used as indicators for the latent constructs

Four-Factor Mediational Model

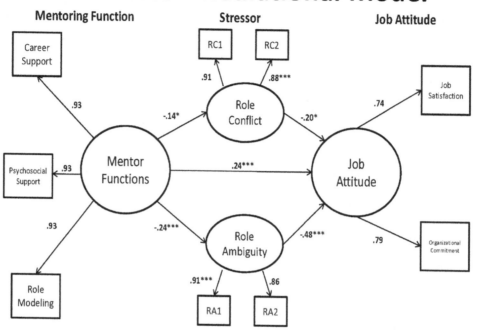

Figure 2. Mediated paths for the four-factor mediational model.

Note: All listed regression weights are standardized. Because path coefficients from the latent variables mentor function and job attitude to their respective indicators were specified, tests of significance are not applicable.

Mentor Functions and Job Attitude, measurement error in the indicator variables was adjusted "by setting the path from the latent variable to the indicator equal to the square root of the scale reliability" (Wayne, Shore, & Liden, 1997, p. 100). In addition, error variance of those indicators was determined by multiplying the value of the indicator by one minus the reliability of the scale (Maruyama, 1998). Overall, the four-factor model adequately fit the data, $\chi^2 (29) = 102.12$, $p < .001$, CFI = .95, TLI = .92, RMSEA = .099. As seen in Figure 2, all of the standardized paths were significant. These results indicate that role conflict and role ambiguity partially mediate the effect of Mentor Functions on Job Attitude but do not completely eliminate the direct relationship. Together, the mediating (i.e., indirect) effect of the work-stress variables accounted for 37% of the relationship between Mentor Functions and Job Attitude. A second model in which the direct path from Mentor Function to Job Attitude was constrained to zero was tested to examine whether the fit of a model that included only the indirect paths (i.e., a fully mediated model) fit significantly worse than the fit of the model that included both direct and indirect paths (i.e., a partially mediated model), $\chi^2_{\text{difference}} (1) = 13.35$, $p < .001$. The fully mediated model demonstrated significantly worse fit than the partially mediated model, indicating that the direct path from Mentor Functions to Job Attitude must remain in the model for the data to demonstrate good fit.

Predictors of Job Satisfaction and Organizational Commitment
for General and Special Education Teachers

The final sample was divided into groups of general education ($N = 206$) and

special education ($N = 54$) teachers. General education and special education teachers

demonstrated a couple of demographic differences. Although the majority of teachers

were female in both groups, special education teachers were significantly more likely

than general education teachers to be female (94% versus 80%), χ^2 (1, $N = 260$) =

6.26, $p = .01$. In addition, special education teachers (55%) were significantly more

likely to be probationary (nontenured) than general education teachers (34%), χ^2 (1, N

$= 257$) $= 7.79$, $p < .01$. In the current sample, special education teachers ($M = 9.30$,

$SD = 7.33$) reported more total years teaching than general education teachers ($M =$

7.41, $SD = 3.95$), F (1, 259) = 6.48, $p = .01$. General education and special education

teachers did not differ in the number of years worked in their current district ($p = .23$),

the student population of their current school ($p = .41$), or the type of school (i.e.,

elementary, middle, or high school) or type of district (i.e., unit K-12, elementary, or

high school) in which they currently teach ($p = .66$ and .97, respectively).

General education ($M = 4.14$, $SD = 0.91$) and special education ($M = 4.07$, SD

$= 0.94$) teachers did not differ in their reported Mentor/Induction support, F (1, 254) =

0.24, $p = .63$, with both groups reporting relatively high levels of support. Although

general education and special education teachers reported equivalent levels of mentor

support, their mentoring experiences did vary in a couple of ways. General education

teachers (87%) more often indicated that their mentoring consisted of participating in

formal meetings compared to special education teachers (76%), χ^2 (1, $N = 258$) = 4.27,

$p < .05$. In contrast, both groups were equally likely to indicate that their mentoring consisted of participating in informal meetings (86% and 91% for general education and special education teachers, respectively), χ^2 (1, $N = 257$) = .78, $p = .38$. General education teachers (57%) were more likely than special education teachers (41%) to report having participated in a mentoring program that was two years in length, whereas special education teachers were more likely to report having participated in a mentoring program that lasted only one year (41% and 59%, for special education and general education teachers, respectively), and neither group reported substantial involvement in mentoring programs lasting longer than two years (0% and 2%, for special education and general education teachers, respectively), χ^2 (2, $N = 260$) = 6.65, $p < .05$. General education (78%) and special education (83%) teachers were equally likely to report that their mentor taught in a similar type of position as them in their first year as a teacher ($p = .44$), but general education teachers (88%) were more likely than special education teachers (70%) to report that their assigned mentor taught in their same school in their first year as a teacher, χ^2 (1, $N = 260$) = 9.86, $p < .01$. General education (65%) and special education (74%) teachers were equally likely to view their mentor as someone who helped them achieve success in their early career as a teacher, χ^2 (1, $N = 260$) = 1.74, $p = .19$.

Multigroup SEM compared the predictors of Job Attitude (indicated by job satisfaction and organizational commitment) among general education versus special education teachers. Correlations between the teachers' scores on the indicators for Mentor Functions (i.e., career support, psychosocial support, role modeling), role conflict, role ambiguity, and the indicators for Job Attitude (i.e., job satisfaction and organizational commitment) are provided in Table 4, separately for general education and special education teachers. Intercorrelations between the variables generally were stronger for general education than for special education teachers (15/21 correlations). However, the magnitude of correlations was significantly different ($p < .05$) across the two groups in only one instance: Job satisfaction was more strongly correlated with organizational commitment among general education than among special education teachers (see Table 4). A series of one-way ANOVAs were conducted to compare general education and special education teachers on all of the study variables (see Table 5). General education teachers reported significantly more role conflict and marginally less job satisfaction than special education teachers, whereas special education teachers reported marginally more role ambiguity.

A series of nested multi-group SEM analyses were performed to test whether the four-factor model (see Figure 2) fit the data equally well for general education and special education teachers (see Table 6). First, the model was fit to the data for general and special education teachers simultaneously with no cross-group equality constraints. The unconstrained model exhibited good fit, $\chi^2 (42) = 74.64, p < .001$; CFI = .98; TLI = .95; RMSEA = .06; path coefficients are provided in Table 6. Next, to test for measurement invariance across groups, a model that constrained the factor loadings of the latent variables to be equal across groups was evaluated against the unconstrained model. Because no difference in the models was revealed, it was concluded that there were no reliable differences in the measurement model between

general education and special education teachers (see Table 6).

Table 4

Correlations of Study Variables for General and Special Education Teachers

Variable	1	2	3	4	5	6	7
1. Vocational support		.82***	.81***	-.11	-.23***	.27***	.34***
2. Psychosocial support	.80***		.80***	-.04	-.16*	.21**	.28***
3. Role modeling	.85***	.83***		-.15*	-.25***	.22**	.35***
4. Role conflict	-.28	-.00	-.21		.54***	-.51***	-.37***
5. Role ambiguity	-.19	-.11	-.10	-.60***		-.57***	-.52***
6. Job satisfaction	.26	.22	.26	-.26	-.31*		.74***
7. Organizational commitment	.30*	.07	.25	-.22	-.28	.50***	

Note. Correlations above the diagonal are for general education teachers ($n = 206$). Correlations below the diagonal are for special education teachers ($n = 54$). Pairwise Ns vary from 182 to 199 for general education and 44 to 50 for special teachers. Bold coefficients differed significantly for general and special education teachers.
$^*p < .05. \ ^{**}p < .01. \ ^{***}p < .001.$

Table 5

One-Way Analyses of Variance for Teacher Type

Variable	General education M (SD)	Special education M (SD)	F	η^2
Career support	3.95 (1.27)	4.11 (1.42)	0.58	.00
Psychosocial support	3.82 (1.39)	3.82 (1.37)	0.00	.00
Role modeling	3.98 (1.31)	4.10 (1.27)	0.32	.00
Role conflict	3.59 (0.80)	3.32 (0.72)	4.59*	.02
Role ambiguity	4.08 (0.76)	4.31 (0.83)	3.42~	.01
Job satisfaction	4.72 (0.97)	5.00 (0.81)	3.43~	.01
Organizational commitment	4.46 (0.89)	4.61 (0.81)	1.01	.00

Note. Pairwise Ns vary from 187 to 200 for general education and 46 to 50 for special education teachers. $\sim p < .10. \ * p < .05.$

Table 6

Multigroup Structural Equation Modeling

Model	χ^2	df	χ^2_Δ	df_Δ	p	CFI	TLI	RMSEA
1. Unconstrained	74.64***	42	N/A	N/A	N/A	.977	.951	.055
2. Measurement weights	77.91***	47	3.27	5	.66	.978	.959	.050
3. Structural weights	98.81**	61	24.17	19	.19	.973	.961	.049

Note. CFI = comparative fit index, TLI = Tucker-Lewis index, RMSEA = root mean square error of approximation. Each consecutive model was tested against the unconstrained model. * $p < .05$. ** $p < .01$. *** $p < .001$.

Next, a model in which the structural weights (path coefficients) were constrained to be equal across groups was examined to test for invariant path coefficients. The fit of this model was good, but was not significantly different than the fit of the unconstrained model. In addition to the fit of the models not differing for general education and special education teachers at the macro level, critical ratio comparisons, used to determine whether individual path coefficients differed across the two groups, revealed no significant differences (see Table 7). These results suggest that, despite the finding that role conflict and role ambiguity accounted for more of the relationship between mentor function and job attitude for general education (45%) compared to special education (18%) teachers, this difference was not significant. Therefore, the model in which the relationship between mentor functions and job attitude are partially mediated by role conflict and role ambiguity fits equally well for both general education and special education teachers.

Table 7

Standardized Structural and Measurement Weights for General Education and

Special Education Teachers

Path		Teacher type	
From	To	General education	Special education
Mentor functions	Role conflict	-.132~	-.186
Mentor functions	Role ambiguity	-.248***	-.181
Mentor functions	Job attitude	.182**	.273
Role conflict	Job attitude	-.234**	.042
Role ambiguity	Job attitude	-.487***	-.372
Mentor functions	Psychosocial support	.897	.882
Mentor functions	Vocational support	.917***	.904***
Mentor functions	Role modeling	.888***	.941***
Role conflict	Role conflict parcel 1	.898	.973
Role conflict	Role conflict parcel 2	.901***	.768***
Role ambiguity	Role ambiguity parcel 1	.923	.890
Role ambiguity	Role ambiguity parcel 2	.849***	.860***
Job attitude	Job satisfaction	.913	.826
Job attitude	Organizational commitment	.813***	.609*

$\sim p < .10.$ $*p < .05.$ $**p < .01.$ $***p < .001.$

CHAPTER 5

DISCUSSION

The current study aimed to provide some level of insight into the mediating
effects of role stressors in the relationship between mentoring and job attitudes.
Specifically, the research sought to determine if reductions in work-related stress, as
measured by role conflict and role ambiguity, account for (i.e., mediate) the positive
relationship between mentoring functions and protégé job attitudes. Previous research
in the human resource and educational literature has shown that mentoring positively
affects job attitude and, in particular, job satisfaction and organizational commitment.
However, the mechanisms through which these positive effects occur are less clear.
Hence, the current study examined the work-related stressors of role conflict and role
ambiguity to determine if there is, in fact, a mediational effect of role stressors on the
relationship between mentoring functions and job attitudes.

As expected, this study found that among teachers in public school districts
across northern Illinois, increased support from one's mentor was associated with less
work-related stress. Specifically, the mentor functions of career support, psychosocial
support, and role modeling were significantly negatively correlated with role
ambiguity, and career support and role modeling were significantly negatively
correlated with role conflict. These findings are consistent with previous research

findings that indicate stress affects teachers' intent to stay in the teaching profession indirectly through job satisfaction and professional commitment (Singh & Billingsley, 1996).

One unexpected finding of the current study was that psychosocial support alone was not significantly related to role conflict. Lankau et al. (2006) found that their sample of mentees in the business field demonstrated a *positive* relationship between psychosocial support and role conflict and role ambiguity, although these authors suggested this positive relationship was due to the high correlations (i.e., multicollinearity) among the mentor function variables. Additional studies also indicated counterintuitive findings regarding social support and job stress (Deelstra et al., 2003; Ganster, Fusilier, & Mayes, 1986; Halbesleben & Buckley, 2004). These studies indicated that receiving support could lead to a perception by mentees that work should be stressful or that receiving this level of support may actually be a threat to the newer employee. These studies utilized business or private sector samples, so perhaps the findings of the current study vary due to the sample of teachers being studied. Teachers are isolated into their own classrooms, so it would seem reasonable that receiving psychosocial support could lead to feelings of less isolation; however, the current study found a lack of significant correlation in either direction when comparing psychosocial support to variables of stress. Further studies may be warranted to examine potential differences in the effects of social support on stress between teachers and private sector employees.

Results of the current study suggest that increased support from a teacher's mentor was associated with increased job satisfaction and organizational commitment, which is consistent with findings from multiple studies that have demonstrated that mentoring is related to positive career and psychosocial outcomes (Boyer & Gillespie, 2000; Whitaker, 2000a; Whitaker, 2000b; Kennedy & Burnstein, 2004; Schlichte et al., 2005; White & Mason, 2006; Thornton et al., 2007). In particular, Whitaker (2000a) identified a positive correlation between mentoring and protégé job satisfaction in her sample of teachers. As expected, higher role conflict and role ambiguity were associated with lower job satisfaction and organizational commitment. Replication of such findings adds to the body of evidence that school districts should find ways to reduce these two work stressors since they have such an effect on job attitude, particularly given the effect of job attitude on teachers' intent to stay in the profession.

The primary goal of the current study as posed by research question one was to examine the mediating role of work-related stress on the relationship between career support, psychosocial support, and role modeling and job satisfaction and organizational commitment. Although a seven-factor model was hypothesized, confirmatory factor analyses supported a four-factor measurement model, wherein the three mentor function variables (i.e., career support, psychosocial support, and role modeling) were combined into one latent construct rather than being treated as three separate constructs as originally hypothesized. Likewise, the two job attitude variables (i.e., job satisfaction and organizational commitment) were combined into one latent construct rather than two as hypothesized. Both of these modifications were supported not only by the improvement in model fit, but also by the high degree of multicollinearity observed among the variables. Lankau and colleagues (2006) also found high correlations among the mentor function scales in their study (range = .52 - .54); however, the degree of multicollinearity was smaller than in the current study (range = .81 - .82). Similarly, Siebert (1999) found high correlations between job satisfaction and organizational commitment. As was the case with the mentor function variables, the degree of multicollinearity among the job attitude variables was higher in the current study compared to previous research. The aforementioned studies consisted of samples outside of education, so there might be reason to suspect that teacher participants differ in their responses compared to nonteacher employees. For instance, there may be a higher degree of overlap in mentoring activities in education which lead to higher correlations in the mentoring functions, and in general, teachers have been found to be a more highly satisfied and committed group than nonteacher groups (Borg & Riding, 1991). Therefore, it could be that differences between teachers and employees in other fields lead to greater multicollinearity in the measured variables. Because the current study only included a sample of teachers, future research including samples of both teachers and employees in other fields is necessary to examine any potential differences.

Results of the current study supported a significant partially mediating role of the studied work-related stressors, role conflict and role ambiguity, in the relationship between mentor functions and job attitude. Results indicated that the latent construct of mentor functions was associated with lower perceptions of role conflict and role ambiguity. The stressors are inversely related to individual perceptions of job satisfaction and organizational commitment. In addition, results supported a significant direct relationship between mentor functions and job attitude. Although this direct relationship exists between latent constructs, the current data does support a mediating mechanism that at least partially explains why mentoring has positive effects on mentee's job attitudes. Within the current sample of teachers, when teachers are faced with increased role demands, they may turn to their mentors in order to reduce work stressors through the provision of career support, role modeling, and psychosocial support. Career support provides assistance in clarification of role expectations and responsibilities, role modeling assists new teachers through the observation of the mentor's behavior, and psychosocial support provides the personal and emotional support new teachers may need when work-related anxieties arise. Extension of this research may focus on which particular stressors occur on a daily, functional level and which stressors are identified as part of role conflict or role ambiguity and are the most troublesome to new teachers. Identifying these types of daily stressors could lead to more practical mentoring activities leading to reduced stress on the job.

Although Lankau et al. (2006) found that the same stress variables were found to be significant mediators, this sample of teachers differs from a sample of business professionals. The literature establishes that teachers specifically are more likely to be satisfied and committed when they perceive a high degree of leadership support (e.g., principal support), and work involvement (Billingsley & Cross, 1992; Rosenholtz, 1989). Gersten et al. (2001) suggests that participation in meaningful, relevant professional development activities leads to higher levels of job satisfaction and commitment. In the school system, levels of professional development may vary but this provision of direct support within the first year or two of the job is typically delivered at high levels during the mentoring and/or induction period.

Although only a partially mediating model was identified in the current study, the effects of stress on teachers, and special education teachers in particular, has been found to lead to burnout and job dissatisfaction (Gersten et al., 2001; Kyriacou, 2001; Strong, 2005; Whitaker, 2000b; Wisniewski, 1997). So although not statistically significant, there is some evidence to suggest that lowering stressors can be accomplished through mentoring functions such as career support, psychosocial support, and role modeling and thus lead to higher levels of job satisfaction and organizational commitment. Higher levels of satisfaction and commitment are then more likely to lead to greater retention in the specific position in a school or to the profession in general. Given that work stress variables accounted for 37% of the relationship between mentor functions and job attitude for the entire sample, there is clearly evidence that stress does, to some extent, affect teacher satisfaction and commitment and can be alleviated through mentoring.

Comparisons of General and Special Educators

Another goal of the current study as posed by research question two was to

identify differences between general education teachers and special education teachers

in the measured variables. An interesting finding between the two groups was that

special educators were more likely to be on probationary status when compared to

their general education peers in the sample; however, special education teachers

reported more total years of teaching. This finding suggests that special education

teachers are less likely to remain in their same employing school district, or in other

words, special educators may be more likely to switch districts throughout their career.

This suggestion is consistent with the finding that organizational commitment was less

strongly correlated with job satisfaction for special educators when compared to

general educators. Billingsley (1993) reported that regardless of how attrition is

measured, special education teachers leave jobs in higher proportions than general

education teachers, and the identified reason is often attributed to work stress. Some

research has demonstrated that attrition in special education is greater than that in

general education (Smith & Ingersoll, 2004), whereas other research has failed to find

statistically significant differences between general education and special education

teachers in their attrition rate (Sindelar, Brownell, and Billingsley, 2010).

Sindelar and colleagues (2010) reported that shortages in special education

consistently have been around 10% for decades, which is higher than shortages found

among general educators. Shortages compounded by attrition among special

educators can lead to districts filling positions with teachers who are not qualified or to inconsistency in delivery of services due to high turnover. If, in fact, special educators are more likely to switch districts due to work-related stress, the need for quality mentoring for this group is even more critical for employing school districts both for quality instructional purposes as well as financial purposes. Future research examining the differences between special education teachers who have moved from one district to another may be beneficial to determine the extent to which stress plays a role in the problem of teacher retention among special educators. Future research may also investigate additional reasons why special education teachers leave their positions. This may require a large enough sample size of special educators to thoroughly examine differences among those that have changed positions and those that have not.

Another difference found between general and special educators was that general educators more often reported that their assigned mentor taught in the same school. Previous research comparing mentoring experiences of general and special education teachers has indicated that there is a strong preference for mentor teachers to teach in the same content area and be within physical proximity of the mentee (Boyer & Gillespie, 2000; Smith & Ingersoll, 2004; Whitaker, 2000a; White & Mason, 2006). Much of this research also has indicated that when mentors and mentees teach in the same content area and are in close physical proximity to each other, more positive outcomes (e.g., higher ratings of job attitude, higher ratings of perceived mentoring effectiveness) are evidenced. However, challenges exist to ensuring that these mentoring conditions are in place. Generally speaking, it is much easier to find a mentor for a beginning teacher who is a general educator than a special educator because there are more general education teachers in a school building than there are special education teachers. Finding a mentor who teaches students with similar disabilities within a similar environment in the same school is difficult. Whitaker found that having a special education teacher mentor was preferred over a general education teacher mentor even if the special education mentor was located in a different building. Whitaker's findings suggest that the current study's findings may be influenced by the fact that special education teachers were more likely to have mentors located at different sites when compared to their general education counterparts. Future research might benefit from considering the role of this variable when examining the effects of mentoring on various outcomes, including work-related stress and job attitude.

The mediating effects of work-stress variables were descriptively different between general and special education teachers in the current sample. As reported, the work-stress variables accounted for 45% of the relationship between mentor functions and job attitude among the general education teachers and only 18% of the relationship among special education teachers in the sample. Although work-related stress appeared to account for more of the relationship between mentor functions and job attitudes among general education compared to special education teachers, the multigroup SEM revealed that the mediational model was not significantly different for each teacher type. These results suggest that, for both groups of teachers, role conflict and role ambiguity only partially explain the relationship between mentoring and job attitude (satisfaction and commitment). The lack of differences in model fit might be explainable by a couple of factors. First, perhaps a larger sample of special education teachers (e.g., a sample that is more comparable in size to the current general education teacher sample) would have led to statistically significant differences in the fit of the mediational model between groups. Second, the relationships between mentoring and job attitude (i.e., job satisfaction and organizational commitment) might be more complex among special education compared to general education teachers. Factors other than work-related stress might more adequately explain the relationship between mentoring and job attitude. Despite these factors, the current study represents the first study to examine potential differences in the mediational effects of work-related stress on the relationships between mentoring and job attitudes in a sample of general and special education teachers.

Study Limitations and Future Implications

A primary limitation of the current study is that self-report measures were utilized to examine variables of interest. Findings may be influenced by common method variance, response consistency effects, or other methodological issues common to self-report methods. A large majority of the reviewed literature on mentoring is similar in terms of how data were collected and analyzed. A particular limitation in the current study is that there may also be a self-selection bias in those who chose to participate in the study. Over 5,500 emails soliciting participation were sent, and only a little over 6% of those responded. It is possible that there is something inherently different about those who chose to participate in the study from those who did not. An additional limitation is that the study was cross-sectional in its design, which did not allow for the interaction of mentoring and role stressors to be analyzed over time. Future research could undertake a more comprehensive look at this through a longitudinal study which might help clarify the developmental relationships between variables.

This study affirms the importance of mentoring and its relationship to job satisfaction and organizational commitment. More importantly, this study does help to identify, to some extent, the importance work stress plays in the lives of new teachers. Mentoring has the potential to contribute to teachers' career outcomes, and finding the right ingredients for the mentoring program is critical to maximize the positive effects of mentoring. This study found that mentoring can be utilized to help employees cope with high levels of role conflict and ambiguity which are prevalent in today's educational workforce.

There is ample evidence to suggest that job satisfaction and organizational commitment are influenced by principal/administrative support (Billingsley, 1993; Billingsley & Cross, 1992; Cross & Billingsley, 1994; Ingersoll, 2003; McKnab, 1983; Platt & Olsen, 1990; Singh & Billingsley, 1996; White & Mason, 2006). Singh and Billingsley specifically identified in their sample of special education teachers that principal support was the strongest influence on job satisfaction and that the second common effect on job satisfaction was role-related problems followed by stress.

Billingsley and Cross found that leadership support was associated with higher levels of organizational commitment. Cross and Billingsley identified that role problems, a form of work-stress, were most strongly related to a lack of principal support when compared to other variables studied. Researchers such as McKnab, Platt, and Olsen identified that lack of administrative support led to greater levels of attrition. Given the importance of principal support in the outcomes of mentoring and measures of job attitude, future research should focus further on the mediational effect that principal support may play in the relationship between mentoring functions and measures of job attitude. Additionally, the principal's role in reducing stress may also be studied to identify job attitude and intent to stay in teaching.

While the current findings support the notion that mentoring benefits mentees, these benefits also translate into benefits for school districts. Districts devote a significant amount of resources to recruitment, induction, and retention of teachers, so creating an induction and mentoring program that leads to outcomes associated with greater retention in a position is financially beneficial. Students also benefit from teachers who stay in their positions since student achievement is highly dependent on the quality of the teacher. Having a novice teacher year after year for some students may lead to lower achievement gains than what may be seen with teachers who are more highly satisfied and committed, and thus have chosen to stay in their positions. Boards of education and administrators understand the importance of retaining teachers but must consider factors and programs related to the retention of teachers (i.e., quality mentoring and induction, type of mentoring program). Similarly, this group of stakeholders would also be interested in what specific components of an induction or mentoring program lead to retention. Future research might examine the extent to which formal mentoring or spontaneous, informal mentoring plays a role in teacher satisfaction, commitment, and stress. Districts employ these mentoring programs which typically include both components, so additional research examining if one versus the other has a greater effect on these measured constructs or the meditational effect of work-stress could lead to better programming at the district level.

Although mentoring demonstrated some important effects on new teachers' psychosocial outcomes, a broader view of induction may be employed in future research investigating the mediating effects of stress on these new teachers' outcomes. Induction is a more comprehensive, multiyear process which aids in helping teachers to adapt to district cultures and learn the academic standards and vision of a district (Wong, 2004). Mentoring is merely one component of an effective induction program. The induction process is viewed as a path of professional development for teachers when they begin their careers. If such a design of induction is employed, the broader mechanisms of induction, including pre-service activities, administrative support, mentoring, and in-service activities, should be analyzed to determine the mediating effects of stress on psychosocial outcomes such as satisfaction and commitment.

REFERENCES

Allen, T. D., Poteet, M. L., Eby, L. T., Lentz, E., & Lima, L. (2004). Career benefits associated with mentoring for protégés: A meta-analysis. *Journal of Applied Psychology, 89*(1), 127-136. doi: 10.1037/0021-9010.89.1.127

Anderson, J. C., & Gerbing, D. W. (1988). Structural equation modeling in practice: A review and recommended two-step approach. *Psychological Bulletin, 103,* 411-423.

Bandura, A. L. (1977). *Social learning theory.* Englewood Cliffs, NJ: Prentice Hall.

Billingsley, B. S. (1993). Teacher retention and attrition in special and general education: A critical review of the literature. *The Journal of Special Education, 27*(2), 137-174.

Billingsley, B. S. (2004). Special education teacher retention and attrition: A critical analysis of the research literature. *The Journal of Special Education, 38*(1), 29-55.

Billingsley, B. S., Carlson, E., & Klein, S. (2004). The working conditions and induction support of early career special educators. *Exceptional Children, 70*(3), 333-347.

Billingsley, B. S., Cross, L. H. (1991). Teachers' decisions to transfer from special to general education. *The Journal of Special Education, 24*(4), 496-511.

Billingsley, B. S., & Cross, L. H. (1992). Predictors of commitment, job satisfaction and intent to stay in teaching: A comparison of general and special educators. *The Journal of Special Education, 25*(4), 453-471.

Boe, E. E. (2006). Long-term trends in the national demand, supply, and shortage of special education teachers. *The Journal of Special Education, 40*(3), 138-150.

Boe, E. E., Bobbitt, S. A., & Cook, L. H. (1997). Whither didst thou go? Retention, reassignment, migration, and attrition of special and general education teachers from a national perspective. *The Journal of Special Education, 30*(4), 371-389.

Boe, E. E., Bobbitt, S. A., Cook, L. H., & Barkanic, G. (1998). *National trends in teacher supply and turnover for special and general education.* Retrieved from ERIC database. (ERIC Document Retrieval Services No. ED426549)

Boe, E. E., Bobbitt, S. A., Cook, L. H., & Weber, A. L. (1997). Why didst thou go? Predictors of retention, transfer, and attrition of special and general education teachers from a national perspective. *The Journal of Special Education, 30*(4), 390-411.

Boe, E. E., Cook, L. H., & Sunderland, R. J. (2008). Teacher turnover: Examining exit attrition, teaching area transfer, and school migration. *Exceptional Children, 75*(1), 7-31.

Borg, M., & Riding, R. (1991). Occupational stress and satisfaction in teaching. *British Educational Research Journal, 17*(3), 263-281.

Bowling, N. A., & Hammond, G. D. (2008). A meta-analytic examination of the construct validity of the Michigan organizational assessment questionnaire job satisfaction subscale. *Journal of Vocational Behavior, 73*(1), 63-77.

Boyer, L., & Gillespie, P. (2000). Keeping the committed: The importance of induction and support programs for new special educators. *Teaching Exceptional Children, 33*(1), 10-15.

Breaux, Al. L., & Wong, H. K. (2003). *New teacher induction: How to train, support, and retain new teachers*. Mountain View, CA: Harry K. Wong Publications, Inc.

Brownell, M. T., Smith, S. W., McNellis, J. R., & Miller, M. D. (1997). Attrition in special education: Why teachers leave the classroom and where they go. *Exceptionality, 7*(3), 143-155.

Cammann, C., Fichman, M., Jenkins, D., & Klesh, J. (1979). *The Michigan Organizational Assessment Questionnaire*. Ann Arbor, MI: University of Michigan.

Cammann, C., Fichman, M., Jenkins, D., & Klesh, J. (1983). Assessing the attitudes and perceptions of organizational members. In S. Seashore, E. Lawler, P. Mirvis, & C. Cammann (Eds.), *Assessing organizational change: A guide to methods, measures and practices* (pp. 71-113). New York, NY: John Wiley.

Castro, S. L., Scandura, T. A., & Williams, E. A. (2006). *Validity of Scandura and Ragins' (1993) multidimensional mentoring measure: An evaluation and refinement*. Manuscript submitted for publication.

Chao, G., Walz, P., & Gardner, P. (1992). Formal and informal mentorships: A comparison on mentoring functions and contrast with nonmentored counterparts. *Personnel Psychology, 45*(3), 619-636.

Cooley, E., & Yovanoff, P. (1996). Supporting professionals at-risk: Evaluating interventions to reduce burnout and improve retention of special educators. *Exceptional Children, 62*(4), 336-355.

Council for Exceptional Children. (2000). *Bright futures for exceptional learners: An action to achieve quality conditions for teaching and learning.* Arlington, VA: Author.

Deelstra, J. T., Peeters, M. C. W., Schaufeli, W. B., Stroebe, W., Zijlstra, F. R. H., & van Doornen, L. P. (2003). Receiving instrumental support at work: When help is not welcome. *Journal of Applied Psychology, 88*, 324-331.

Egan, T. M., & Song, Z. (2008). Are facilitated mentoring programs beneficial? A randomized experimental field study. *Journal of Vocational Behavior, 72*, 351-362. doi: 10.1016/j.jvb.2007.10.009

Feaster, R. (2002). Mentoring the new teacher. *Journal of School Improvement, 3*(2), 1-6.

Fields, D. L. (2002). *Taking the measure of work: A guide to validated scales for organizational research and diagnosis.* Thousand Oaks, CA: Sage.

Forbes, C. T. (2004). Peer mentoring in the development of beginning secondary science teachers: Three case studies. *Mentoring and Tutoring, 12*(2), 219-238. doi: 10.1080/1361126042000239956

Fore, C., Martin, C., & Bender. W. N. (2002). Teacher burnout in special education: The causes and the recommended solutions. *High School Journal, 86*(1), 36-44.

Fletcher, S. H., & Barrett, A. (2004). Developing effective beginning teachers through mentor-based induction. *Mentoring and Tutoring, 12*(3), 321-333. doi: 10.1080/030910042000275936

Fletcher, S. H., & Strong, M. A. (2009). Full-release and site-based mentoring of new elementary grade teachers: An analysis of changes in student achievement. *The New Educator, 5*, 329-341.

Fletcher, S., Strong, M., & Villar, A. (2008). An investigation of the effects of variations in mentor-based induction on the performance of students in California. *Teachers College Record, 110*(10), 2271-2289.

Gall, M. D., Gall, J. P., & Borg, W. R. (2007). *Educational research: An introduction* (8th ed.). Boston, MA: Pearson Education.

Ganster, D. C., Fusilier, M. R., & Mayes, B. T. (1986). Role of social support in the experience of stress at work. *Journal of Applied Psychology, 71*, 102-110.

Gehrke, R. S., & Murri, N. (2006). Beginning special educators' intent to stay in special education: Why they like it here. *Teacher Education and Special Education, 29*(3), 179-190.

Gerston, R., Keating, T., Yovanoff, P., and Harniss, M. K. (2001). Working in special education: Factors that enhance special educators' intent to stay. *Exceptional Children, 67*(4), 549-567.

Halbesleben, J. R. B., & Buckley, M. R. (2004). Burnout in organizational life. *Journal of Management, 30*, 859-879.

Hope, W. C. (1999). Principals' orientation and induction activities as factors in teacher retention. *The Clearing House, 73*(1), 54-56.

Hu, L., & Bentler, P. M. (1999). Cutoff criteria for fit indexes in covariance structure analysis: Conventional criteria versus new alternatives. *Structural Equation Modeling: A Multidisciplinary Journal, 6,* 1-55.

Ingersoll, R., & Kralik, J. M. (2004). *The impact of mentoring on teacher retention: What the research says.* Denver, CO: Education Commission of the States.

Kammeyer-Mueller, J. D., & Judge, T. A. (2007). A quantitative review of the mentoring research: Test of a model. *Journal of Vocational Behavior, 72,* 269-283. doi: 10.1016/j.jvb.2007.09.006

Kennedy, V. & Burstein, N. (2004). An induction program for special education teachers. *Teacher Education and Special Education, 27*(4), 444-447.

Kilburg, G. M., & Hancock, T. (2006). Addressing sources of collateral damage in four mentoring programs. *Teachers College Record, 108*(7), 1321-1338.

Kline, R. B. (1998). *Principles and practice of Structural Equation Modeling.* New York: The Guilford Press.

Kram, K. E. (1985). *Mentoring at work: Developmental relationships in organizational life.* Glenview, IL: Scott, Foresman.

Kyriacou, C. (1987). Teacher stress and burnout: An international review. *Educational Research, 29*, 146-152.

Kyriacou, C. (2001). Teacher stress: Directions for future research. *Educational Review, 53*(1), 27-35. doi: 10.1080/00131910120033628

Lam, S. S. K. (1998). Test-retest reliability of the Organizational Commitment Questionnaire. *The Journal of Social Psychology, 138*(6), 787-788.

Lankau, M. J., Carlson, D. S., & Nielson, T. R. (2006). The mediating influence of role stressors in the relationship between mentoring and job attitudes. *Journal of Vocational Behavior, 68,* 308-322. doi: 10.1016/j.jvb.2005.06.001

Lauritzen, P. (1986). *Comprehensive assessment of service needs for special education.* Madison, WI: Wisconsin Department of Public Instruction.

Luekens, M. T., Lyter, D. M., & Fox, E. E. (2004). *Teacher attrition and mobility: Results from the Teacher Follow-up Survey, 2000-01* (NCES Publication No. 2004-301). Washington, DC: National Center for Education Statistics, U.S. Department of Education.

Maruyama, G. M. (1998). *Basics of structural equation modeling.* Thousand Oaks, CA: Sage.

Marvel, J., Lyter, D. M., Peltola, P., Strizek, G. A., & Morton, B. A. (2006). *Teacher attrition and mobility: Results from the 2004-05 teacher follow-up study* (NCES Publication No. 2007-307). U.S. Department of Education, National Center for Education Statistics. Washington, DC: U.S. Government Printing Office.

McKnab, P. (1983). *Special education personnel attrition in Kansas, 1976-1982: A summary of attrition rates and an analysis of reasons for quitting.* Retrieved from ERIC database (ERIC Document Retrieval Services No. ED238231)

McKnab, P. (1995). *Attrition rates of special education personnel in Kansas: 1993-94 to 1994-95.* Retrieved from ERIC database (ERIC Document Retrieval Services No. ED380977)

Melnick, S. A., & Meister, D. G. (2008). A comparison of beginning and experienced teacher's concerns. *Educational Research Quarterly, 31*(3), 39-56.

Mowday, R. T., Porter, L. M., & Steers, R. M. (1982). *Employee-organization linkables: The psychology of commitment, absenteeism, and turnover.* New York, NY: Academic Press.

Noe, R. A. (1988). An investigation of the determinants of successful assigned mentoring relationships. *Personnel Psychology, 41,* 457-479.

Odell, S. J., & Ferraro, D. P. (1992). Teacher mentoring and teacher retention. *Journal of Teacher Education, 43*(3), 200-204.

Platt, J. M., & Olson, J. (1990). Why teachers are leaving special education. *Teacher Education and Special Education, 13*(3,4), 192-196.

Porter, L. W., & Smith, F. J. (1970). *The etiology of organizational commitment.* Unpublished paper, University of California at Irvine.

Porter, L. S., Steers, R. M., Mowday, R. T., & Boulian, P. V. (1974). Organizational commitment, job satisfaction, and turnover among psychiatric technicians. *Journal of Applied Psychology, 59*(5), 603-609.

Quinn, R. J., & Andrews, B. D. (2004). The struggles of first-year teachers: Investigating support mechanisms. *The Clearing House, 77*(4), 164-168.

Rizzo, J. R., House, R. J., & Lirtzman, S. I. (1970). Role conflict and ambiguity in complex organizations. *Administrative Science Quarterly, 15,* 150-163.

Rosenholtz, S. J. (1989). Workplace conditions that affect teacher quality and commitment: Implications for teacher induction programs. *The Elementary School Journal, 89,* 421-439.

Scandura, T. A. (1992). Mentorship and career mobility: An empirical investigation. *Journal of Organizational Behavior, 13,* 169-174.

Scherff, L., & Hahs-Vaughn, D. L., (2008). What we know about English language arts teachers: An analysis of the 1999-2000 SASS and 2000-2001 TFS databases. *English Education, 40*(3), 174-200.

Schlichte, J. Yssel, N., & Merbler, J. (2005). Pathways to burnout: Case studies in teacher isolation and alienation. *Preventing School Failure, 50*(1), 35-40.

Seery, B. M. (1990). *Generalized and specific sources of job satisfaction related to attrition and retention of teachers of behavior-disordered and severely emotionally disturbed students in Georgia.* Retrieved from ProQuest Dissertation Abstracts. (AAT 9112211).

Seibert, S. (1999). The effectiveness of facilitated mentoring: A longitudinal quasi-experiment. *Journal of Vocational Behavior, 54,* 483-502.

Singh, K., & Billingsley, B. S. (1996). Intent to stay in teaching: Teachers of students with emotional disorders versus other special educators. *Remedial and Special Education, 17*(1), 37-47.

Smith, T. M., & Ingersoll, R. M. (2004). What are the effects of induction and mentoring on beginning teacher turnover? *American Educational Research Journal, 41*(3), 681-714.

Spector, P. E. (1985). Measurement of human service staff satisfaction: Development of the job satisfaction survey. *American Journal of Community Psychology, 13*, 693-713.

Strong, M. (2005). Teacher induction, mentoring, and retention: A summary of the research. *The New Educator, 1*, 181-198. doi: 10.1080/15476880590966295.

Thornton, B. Peltier, G., and Medina, R. (2007). Reducing the special education teacher shortage. *The Clearing House, 80*(5), 233-238.

Waters, L. (2004). Protégé-mentor agreement about the provision of psychosocial support: The mentoring relationship, personality, and workload. *Journal of Vocational Behavior, 65,* 519-532. doi: 10.1016/j.jvb.2003.10.004

Wayne, S. J., Shore, L. M., & Liden, R. C. (1997). Perceived organizational support and leader-member exchange: A social exchange perspective. *Academy of Management Journal, 40,* 82-111.

Whitaker, S. D. (2000a). Mentoring beginning special education teachers and the relationship to attrition. *Exceptional Children, 66*(4), 546-566.

Whitaker, S. D. (2000b). What do first-year special education teachers need? Implications for induction programs. *Teaching Exceptional Children, 33*(1), 28-36.

Whitaker, S. D. (2003). Needs of beginning special education teachers: Implications for teacher education. *Teacher Education and Special Education, 26*(2), 106-117.

White, M., & Mason, C. (2006). Components of a successful mentoring program for beginning special education teachers: Perspectives from new teachers and mentors. *Teacher Education and Special Education, 29*(3), 191-201.

Wisniewski, L., & Gargiulo, R. M. (1997). Occupational stress and burnout among special educators: A review of the literature. *The Journal of Special Education, 31*(3), 325-346.

Wong, H. K. (2004). Induction programs that keep new teachers teaching and improving. *NASSP Bulletin, 88*(638), 41-58.

APPENDICES

APPENDIX A

RECRUITMENT LETTER

Dear Education Colleague,

I am a doctoral graduate student at Northern Illinois University in the department of educational leadership. As part of the degree requirements, I am completing my dissertation and am currently recruiting participants for my study. The topic of the study is the effects of mentoring on measures of job attitude and how work-stress plays a role in this relationship.

I am seeking **general education and special education teachers** who are within their **second to tenth year** in their employing public school district and who had a mentor in their first year of employment with their current district. A mentor is defined as an individual (typically a more senior member of your organization) who has advanced experience and knowledge and who is committed to the enhancement and support of your career.

Participation in this study requires completion of electronic questionnaires found at the linked survey below. Participation is voluntary and may be withdrawn at any time. All individual data and identifying information will be confidential and will only be seen by me, the researcher. Since the information will be confidential, there is no threat to your reputation or employment in your district. Individual responses will not be published as all responses will be aggregated for data analysis. If you choose to participate, you will have the option of requesting that a summary of research results are provided to you upon completion of the study.

Your participation in this study is very much appreciated. Upon completion of the survey, your name will be placed in a drawing to win one of ten $25 Visa gift cards. Winners will be notified via email.

If you meet the criteria indicated above and are willing to participate, click on the link below. You will be taken to a consent for participation page which will provide more details about the study and participation procedures. The survey will take approximately 10 to 20 minutes. Thank you in advance.

Greg Rabenhorst

Insert link to survey.com

APPENDIX B

CONSENT FOR PARTICIPATION

CONSENT FOR PARTICIPATION

Thank you for your willingness to consider participation in this research study. The following information details the purpose of the study, the procedures employed, confidentiality, and participation.

Study Purpose: This study investigates the relationship of mentoring and psychosocial outcome measures such as stress and job attitude.

Research Procedures: You will be asked to respond to several questionnaires based on your experience in a mentoring program and your experience and feelings related to your current job. All questions have response options to choose from.

Upon completion of each page of the survey, you will be prompted to continue to the next page of the survey. You will receive notification of completion at the end of the survey.

To show appreciation for your time, upon survey completion you will be entered into a drawing to win one of ten (10) $25 Visa gift cards. The study will take approximately 10-20 minutes.

Research Risks: Participation will pose no risk of injury or need for medical treatment.

Research Benefits: Participation in this study will assist in adding to the research literature relevant to the potential benefits of mentoring as an intervention for first-year teachers.

Confidentiality: Only the researcher and research assistants will have access to your data. All data will be securely stored electronically. Technology used for data collection will be password protected. Printed data will be kept in locked cabinets used only for the research project. The locked cabinet will be housed with the researcher. Your data will be combined with the data from other teachers participating in this study and only group data will be reported. Further, the researcher will not reveal any information that you provide in any proceedings which attempt to force disclosure in order to identify you.

Participation: Participation is voluntary. You have the right not to answer any specific question as well as to withdraw from the study at any time. A decision not to participate will involve no penalty or loss of benefits to which you are otherwise entitled. Your acknowledgment of consent at the bottom of this page means that you are willing to take part in the study. **By electronically consenting you do not give up any rights to which you are legally entitled.**

Contacts: Further information about the study may be obtained by calling the researcher, Greg Rabenhorst, Northern Illinois University Doctoral Candidate, Department of Educational Leadership at 815-762-0447 between 8:00AM and 4:30PM CST. Questions or concerns about participant protection should be addressed to the Office for Research Compliance, Northern Illinois University, DeKalb, Illinois, 60115, at 815-753-8588 between 8:00AM and 4:30PM CST.

Voluntary Consent and Certification: I have read the above statements. I understand the purpose of the study as well as the benefits of the study as stated. I understand that I can withdraw from the study at any time for any reason. I give my informed consent to be a participant in this study. I understand that at this time I can print this consent form if I choose to retain a copy.

Participant Name:
Date:

By checking this box, I acknowledge consent for participation: ☐

Check here only if you wish to receive a summary of research results from this study upon its completion: ☐

APPENDIX C

DEMOGRAPHICS

DEMOGRAPHICS

This questionnaire asks questions about your employment background and experience in a mentoring program. For purposes of this study, a mentor is defined as an individual (typically a more senior member of your school/school district) who has advanced experience and knowledge and who is committed to the enhancement and support of your career. A mentoring program is defined as a required component of induction that you participated in during your first year of employment with your *current* school/school district.

1. Indicate your primary teaching position:
   General Education Teacher / Special Education Teacher

2. Gender: Female / Male

3. Total Number of Years Teaching (count the current year as one year of teaching):

   _____

4. Total Number of Years Teaching *in your current employing district* (count the current year as one year of teaching):
   1/2/3/4/5/6/7/8/9/10/11+

5. Tenure status:
   Tenured / Probationary (nontenured)

6. Type of school you currently working in:
   Elementary (including pre-K) / Middle School-Jr High / High School

7. Type of school *district* you currently work in:
   Unit (K-12) / Elementary / High School

8. Indicate the approximate student population of the school you currently work in:
   0-199 / 200-499 / 500-799 / 800-1199 / 1200+

9. I was required to participate (or chose to participate if not required) in a mentoring program when I began working in my *current* employing district.
   YES NO

10. I was assigned a mentor in my first year of teaching with my *current* employing district.
    YES NO

    IF NO, SKIP LOGIC TO END OF SURVEY

11. Indicate the length of the mentoring program in your current employing district when you were involved in the program.
    1 year / 2 years / More than 2 years

12. Mentoring consisted of participating in formal meetings (i.e., presentations, seminars, workshops, etc.) that were established by my employing school/district.
    YES   NO

13. Indicate the approximate number of formal mentoring meetings you were required to participate in <u>within your first year</u> of employment:
    1-3, 4-6, 7-9, 10 or more, Not applicable

14. Mentoring consisted of participating in informal meetings/sessions just between you and your assigned mentor.
    YES   NO

15. Indicate the approximate number of informal mentoring sessions you participated in with your mentor <u>within your first year</u> of employment:
    1-5, 6-10, 11-15, 16-20, 21-25, 26-30, 31-35, 36-40, 40 or more

16. Mentoring was a valuable part of my early career development.
    1=Very Strongly Disagree
    2=Strongly Disagree
    3=Disagree
    4=Agree
    5=Strongly Agree
    6=Very Strongly Agree

17. My assigned mentor taught in a similar type of position as me in my first year as a teacher (e.g., if you are a special education teacher, your mentor also was a special education teacher; if you are a general education teacher, your mentor was also a general education teacher in the same grade level or subject area).
    Yes / No

18. My assigned mentor taught in the same school as me in my first year as a teacher.
    Yes / No

19. Even today, I view my mentor as someone who helped me achieve success in my early career as a teacher.
    1 = Very Strongly Disagree
    2 = Strongly Disagree
    3 = Disagree
    4 = Agree
    5 = Strongly Agree
    6 = Very Strongly Agree

20. If you had previous experience in another school/district prior to working in your current employing district, did you have a formal mentoring experience?
YES   NO   Not Applicable

Total Mentoring/Induction Support

For each of the following statements, think back to your mentoring experience in your ***first year of teaching*** with your ***current employing school/district***. For each statement, select the response that most applies to how you felt during your mentoring and induction experience in your current job. Please indicate the degree of your agreement or disagreement with each statement by selecting one of the six alternatives below each statement.

1. My assigned mentor helped me find the books and/or supplies that I needed to start the school year.

2. I had no idea how to manage all of the required paperwork (attendance, correcting papers, recording grades, tracking students' progress).

3. I learned some useful classroom management techniques from my assigned mentor.

4. I felt like no one in my school was willing to listen to my problems.

5. I had the opportunity to plan lessons and/or units with my assigned mentor.

6. There was no one at my school with whom I could openly discuss my teaching philosophies and/or new ideas about teaching.

7. I received help from my assigned mentor with tasks like making copies, obtaining AV equipment, preparing for conferences, etc.

8. I had the opportunity to observe my assigned mentor while he or she was teaching.

9. I received no help or direction in planning lessons that would cover the material required to cover the state standards adequately.

10. I received support and encouragement from my assigned mentor.

11. I could go to my assigned mentor to discuss ideas that I had for creating innovative lessons or units.

12. I received very little or no help in obtaining materials and supplies to use in my classroom.

13. If I didn't understand how a policy or procedure in my school or in the district worked, I could go to my assigned mentor for clarification.

14. No one observed my teaching and/or gave me constructive feedback except my formal evaluator.

15. I received moral support from my assigned mentor.

16. I received very little help in obtaining books or other resources that were necessary for me to teach adequately.

17. I could get advice on adapting my lessons plans to meet the needs of my students from my assigned mentor.

18. If could go to my assigned mentor when I needed to know how to handle certain things (field trips, parent conferences, discipline referrals, etc.).

19. There was no one I could go to for advice when things went badly with a lesson or classroom management.

20. I could honestly discuss any problems I may have had in the classroom with my assigned mentor.

1 = Very Strongly Disagree
2 = Strongly Disagree
3 = Disagree
4 = Agree
5 = Strongly Agree
6 = Very Strongly Agree

Mentoring Support by Function

For each of the following statements, select the number that most applies to how you felt during your mentoring and induction experience in your current job. Please indicate the degree of your agreement or disagreement with each statement by selecting one of the six alternatives below each statement.

1. My mentor took a personal interest in my career.

2. My mentor helped me coordinate professional goals.

3. My mentor devoted special time and consideration to my career.

4. I shared personal problems with my mentor.

5. I exchanged confidences with my mentor.

6. I considered my mentor to be my friend.

7. I tried to model my behavior after my mentor.

8. I admired my mentor's ability to motivate others.

9. I respected my mentor's ability to teach others.

1 = Very Strongly Disagree
2 = Strongly Disagree
3 = Disagree
4 = Agree
5 = Strongly Agree
6 = Very Strongly Agree

Work-Related Stress

Listed below is a series of statements that represent possible feelings that individuals might have about their current job or work environment.   With respect to your own feelings about your current job or work environment, please indicate the degree of your agreement or disagreement with each statement by selecting one of the six alternatives below each statement.

1. I have things to do that should be done differently.

2. I have to buck a rule or a policy in order to carry out an assignment.

3. I receive incompatible requests from two or more people.

4. I do things that are apt to be accepted by one person and not accepted by others.

5. I work on unnecessary things.

6. I work with two or more groups who operate quite differently.

7. I receive assignments without the manpower to complete them.

8. I receive assignments without adequate resources and materials to execute them.

9. I know exactly what is expected of me.

10. I know that I have divided my time properly.

11. Explanation is clear of what has to be done.

12. I feel certain about how much authority I have.

13. I know what my responsibilities are.

14. Clear, planned goals and objectives exist for my job.

1 = Very Strongly Disagree
2 = Strongly Disagree
3 = Disagree
4 = Agree
5 = Strongly Agree
6 = Very Strongly Agree

Job Satisfaction

Listed below are statements that represent possible feelings that individuals might have about their current job. With respect to your own feelings about your current job, please indicate the degree of your agreement or disagreement with each statement by selecting one of the six alternatives below each statement.

1. All in all, I am satisfied with my job.

2. In general, I don't like my job.

3. In general, I like working here.

1 = Very Strongly Disagree
2 = Strongly Disagree
3 = Disagree
4 = Agree
5 = Strongly Agree
6 = Very Strongly Agree

Organizational Commitment

Listed below is a series of statements that represent possible feelings that individuals might have about the company or organization for which they work. With respect to your own feelings about the particular school for which you are now working, please indicate the degree of your agreement or disagreement with each statement by selecting one of the six alternatives below each statement.

1. I am willing to put in a great deal of effort beyond that normally expected in order to help this school be successful.

2. I talk up this school to my friends as a great organization to work for.

3. I would accept almost any type of job assignment in order to keep working for this school.

4. I find that my values and the school's values are very similar.

5. I am proud to tell others that I am part of this school.

6. This school really inspires the very best in me in the way of job performance.

7. I am extremely glad that I chose this school to work for over others I was considering at the time I joined.

8. I really care about the fate of this school.

9. For me, this is the best of all possible schools for which to work.

1 = Very Strongly Disagree
2 = Strongly Disagree
3 = Disagree
4 = Agree
5 = Strongly Agree
6 = Very Strongly Agree

APPENDIX D

RECRUITMENT LETTER—FOLLOW-UP #1

Dear Education Colleague,

I am a doctoral graduate student at Northern Illinois University in the department of educational leadership. A couple of weeks ago, I emailed you regarding participation in my dissertation research. I want to extend my appreciation to you if you have participated in this study. If you have not yet participated, I would like to again ask you to consider participating. The topic of the study is the effects of mentoring on measures of job attitude and how work-stress plays a role in this relationship.

I am seeking **general education and special education teachers** who are within their **second to tenth year** in their employing public school district and who had a mentor in their first year of employment with their current district. A mentor is defined as an individual (typically a more senior member of your organization) who has advanced experience and knowledge and who is committed to the enhancement and support of your career.

Participation in this study requires completion of electronic questionnaires found at the linked survey below. Participation is voluntary and may be withdrawn at any time. All individual data and identifying information will be confidential and will only be seen by me, the researcher. Since the information will be confidential, there is no threat to your reputation or employment in your district. Individual responses will not be published as all responses will be aggregated for data analysis. If you choose to participate, you will have the option of requesting that a summary of research results are provided to you upon completion of the study.

Your participation in this study is very much appreciated. Upon completion of the survey, your name will be placed in a drawing to win one of ten $25 Visa gift cards. Winners will be notified via email.

If you meet the criteria indicated above and are willing to participate, click on the link below. You will be taken to a consent for participation page which will provide more details about the study and participation procedures. The survey will take approximately 10 to 20 minutes. Thank you in advance.

Greg Rabenhorst

Insert link to survey.com

APPENDIX E

RECRUITMENT LETTER—FOLLOW-UP #2

Dear Education Colleague,

Several weeks ago, I contacted you regarding participation in my dissertation research which aims to study the effects of mentoring on measures of job attitude and how work-stress plays a role in this relationship. As I have not yet reached a sufficient sample size, I am asking once again for your volunteer participation in my study.

I am seeking **general education and special education teachers** who are within their **second to tenth year** in their employing public school district and who had a mentor in their first year of employment with their current district. A mentor is defined as an individual (typically a more senior member of your organization) who has advanced experience and knowledge and who is committed to the enhancement and support of your career.

Participation in this study requires completion of electronic questionnaires found at the linked survey below. Participation is voluntary and may be withdrawn at any time. All individual data and identifying information will be confidential and will only be seen by me, the researcher. Since the information will be confidential, there is no threat to your reputation or employment in your district. Individual responses will not be published as all responses will be aggregated for data analysis. If you choose to participate, you will have the option of requesting that a summary of research results are provided to you upon completion of the study.

Your participation in this study is very much appreciated. Upon completion of the survey, your name will be placed in a drawing to win one of ten $25 Visa gift cards. Winners will be notified via email.

If you meet the criteria indicated above and are willing to participate, click on the link below. You will be taken to a consent for participation page which will provide more details about the study and participation procedures. The survey will take approximately 10 to 20 minutes. Thank you once again for considering your participation in this study.

Greg Rabenhorst
Graduate Student
Northern Illinois University

Insert link to survey.com

APPENDIX F

SUPPLEMENTAL SEM ANALYSES

    Although the hypothesized seven-factor and the modified five-factor measurement models demonstrated poor fit, the structural models were fitted on these larger models as supplemental analyses.

    Overall, the originally hypothesized seven-factor model in which the relationships between the mentor functions of career support, psychosocial support, and role modeling with the job attitudes of job satisfaction and organizational commitment were mediated through the work stressors role conflict and role ambiguity demonstrated adequate fit, χ^2 (131) = 327.94, $p < .001$, CFI = .96, TLI = .94, RMSEA = .08. In addition, 11 of the 16 structural paths of interest were nonsignificant at $p < .05$. These results suggest that the hypothesized model was a poor fit for the data at both a measurement and structural level.

    The reduced five-factor structural model, in which the work stressors role conflict and role ambiguity were predicted to mediate the relationship between mentor function (indicated by career support, psychosocial support, and role modeling) and job satisfaction and organizational commitment also was tested. Seven out of the eight structural paths of interest were significant at $p < .05$, and the fit indices revealed adequate fit, χ^2 (60) = 170.65, $p < .001$, CFI = .96, TLI = .94, RMSEA = .08.

Lightning Source UK Ltd.
Milton Keynes UK
UKOW06f1841061113

220585UK00010B/632/P